PROTECTION OF ASSETS

APPLICATIONS

PROTECTION OF ASSETS

APPLICATIONS

ASIS INTERNATIONAL
Advancing Security Worldwide®

ASIS International | 1625 Prince Street | Alexandria, VA 22314 USA | *www.asisonline.org*

ISBN 978-1-934904-20-6

Protection of Assets is furnished with the understanding that the publisher is not engaged in rendering legal, accounting, or other professional services. It is designed as a ready reference and guide to the covered subjects. While every effort has been made to ensure accuracy of contents herein, it is not an official publication and the publisher can assume no responsibility for errors or omissions.

Printed in the United States of America.

10 9 8 7 6 5 4 3

ACKNOWLEDGMENTS

ASIS International (ASIS), the world's leading society for security professionals, originally founded in 1955 as the American Society for Industrial Security, acquired *Protection of Assets* in December 2003. The acquisition of this work underscores the Society's leadership role in professional education. It is the sincere desire of ASIS and its editorial staff to continue to enhance the value of this important reference.

Protection of Assets, which has been in existence since 1974, is recognized as the premier reference for security professionals and the publisher wishes to acknowledge the two founding authors and subsequent editors.

Timothy J. Walsh, CPP **Richard J. Healy, CPP**

Timothy L. Williams, CPP
Managing Editor

Editorial Associates

David G. Aggleton, CPP
Milton E. Moritz, CPP
Mike Hodge, J.D.
Sanford Sherizon, Ph.D., CISSP
Timothy J. Walsh, CPP, Editor Emeritus

As we move forward, confronted with issues that present a challenge to the security industry, our mission is to ensure that *Protection of Assets* provides the strategic solutions necessary to help professionals meet the demands of the 21st century and beyond. We also pledge to assemble a group of subject matter experts who will enhance this reference as necessary to achieve our mission.

Michael E. Knoke, CPP
Managing Editor

Eva Giercuszkiewicz, MLS, Project Manager
Evangeline Pappas, Production Manager
Peter E. Ohlhausen, Technical Editor

PREFACE

OBJECTIVES OF *PROTECTION OF ASSETS*

Protection of Assets (POA) is intended for a security professional to find current, accurate, and practical treatment of the broad range of asset protection subjects, strategies, and solutions in a single source.

The need for such a comprehensive resource is quite widespread according to the editors, writers, and many professional colleagues whose advice has been sought in compiling this text. The growing size and frequency of all forms of asset losses, coupled with the related increasing cost and complexity of countermeasures selection, demand a systematic and unified presentation of protection doctrine in all relevant areas, as well as standards and specifications as they are issued. Of course, it would be presumptuous to assume that any small group of authors could present such material unaided. It is, therefore, a fundamental objective of *Protection of Assets* to draw upon as large a qualified source base as can be developed. The writers, peer reviewers, and editors attempt to distill from the available data, common or recurrent characteristics, trends, and other factors, which identify or signal valid protection strategies. The objective is to provide a source document where information on any protection problem can be obtained.

READERSHIP

Protection of Assets is intended for a wide readership: all security professionals and business managers with asset protection responsibility. The coherent discussion and pertinent reference material in each subject area should help the reader conduct unique research that is effective and organized. Of particular significance are the various forms, matrices, and checklists that give the reader a practical start toward application of the security theory to his or her own situation. *POA* also serves as a central reference for students pursuing a program in security or asset protection.

DIALOGUE

We hope that *Protection of Assets* becomes an important source of professional insight for those who read it and that it stimulates serious dialogue between and among security professionals. Any reader who is grappling with an unusual, novel, or difficult security problem and would appreciate the opinions of others is encouraged to write a succinct statement describing the problem and send it to us at ASIS [protectionofassets@asisonline.org]. At the reader's request his identity will not be disclosed, but the problem will be published with invitations for comment. Readers are also encouraged to communicate agreement or disagreement with strategies or applications recommended in *POA* and to suggest alternatives. We reserve the right to publish or refrain from publishing submitted material. The editors also solicit statements of reader opinion on matters of asset protection policy in which a cross-sectional view would be helpful.

SUPPLEMENTAL TRAINING

Readers with supervisory or management responsibility for other security and asset protection personnel will find *POA* to be a useful resource from which to assign required readings. Such readings could be elements of a formal training syllabus and could be assigned as part of related course sessions.

With all these objectives in mind, we present to you *Protection of Assets*, in the sincere belief it will enhance your expertise in the security field.

Michael E. Knoke, CPP
Managing Editor

CONTRIBUTORS

The success of this publication is directly related to the peer review process recognized by most professions. Security professionals, members of academia, and other subject matter experts were involved in contributing current information, conducting research, reviewing submissions, and providing constructive comments so that we are able to provide a publication that is recognized as the "go to" reference for security professionals worldwide.

It is with sincere appreciation that I wish to thank the below-named individuals who contributed to *Protection of Assets*.

Teresa M. Abrahamsohn, CPP
Sean A. Ahrens, CPP
Marene N. Allison
Randy I. Atlas, CPP
George J. Barletta, CPP
Mark H. Beaudry, CPP
Regis W. Becker, CPP
Brent Belcoff, CPP
Howard J. Belfor, CPP
Adolfo M. Benages, CPP
Lawrence K. Berenson, CPP
Alexander E. Berlonghi
Raymond J. Bernard, PSP
Henri A. Berube
Martin T. Biegelman, J.D.
Daniel E. Bierman, CPP, PSP
Patrick C. Bishop, CPP
Dennis R. Blass, CPP, PSP
Keith C. Blowe, CPP
Paul F. Boyarin, CPP, PCI
Tom Boyer
Pete Brake, Jr., CPP
Darryl R. Branham, CPP
Joseph P. Buckley, III
Jason Caissie, CPP, PSP
Lucien G. Canton, CPP
James P. Carino, Jr., CPP
Sue Carioti
James S. Cawood, CPP, PCI, PSP
Steve Chambers, CPP, PSP
Richard E. Chase, CPP
John C. Cholewa, III, CPP
Tom M. Conley, CPP
Geoffrey T. Craighead, CPP
Michael A. Crane, J.D., CPP
Bruce A. Dean, CPP
Fritz X. Delinski
Edward P. De Lise, CPP
David A. Dobbins, PSP
Colin Doniger, CPP, PSP
Clifford E. Dow, CPP
Christina M. Duffey, CPP
Brandon Dunlap
Nick Economou
Cheryl D. Elliott, CPP, PCI
James W. Ellis, CPP, PSP
William R. Etheridge
Gregory Alan Ewing, CPP, PSP
Kenneth G. Fauth, CPP
Lawrence J. Fennelly
Donald J. Fergus
Eugene F. Ferraro, CPP, PCI
James H. Fetzer, III, CPP
Michael T. Flachs, CPP
Linda F. Florence, Ph.D., CPP
Richard H. Frank, CPP
Kenneth M. Freeman, CPP
Peter J. French, CPP
Mary Lynn Garcia, CPP
John W. Gehrlein, CPP
Eva Giercuszkiewicz, MLS
Gregory A. Gilbert, CPP
Frederick G. Giles, CPP
Timothy D. Giles, CPP, PSP
David H. Gilmore, CPP
Christopher Giusti, CPP
Leo Gonnering, PSP
Brian D. Gouin, PSP
Richard P. Grassie, CPP
Benjamin P. Greer
Steven R. Harris
Ronald D. Heil, CPP
Ed Heisler, CPP, PSP
Richard J. Heffernan, CPP
Chris A. Hertig, CPP

William T. Hill, CPP
Ronald W. Hobbs, CPP
Mark D. Hucker, CPP
W. Geoffrey Hughes, PCI
John L. Hunepohl
Gregory L. Hurd, CPP
Gregory W. Jarpey, PSP
Sheila D. Johnson, CPP, PSP
Thomas R. Jost
Diane Horn Kaloustian
Cathy M. Kimble, CPP
R. Michael Kirchner, CPP
Glen W. Kitteringham, CPP
Michael E. Knoke, CPP
Terrence J. Korpal
James M. Kuehn, CPP
David Lam, CPP
Rich LaVelle, PSP
Robert F. Leahy, CPP, PSP
Robert E. Lee
Jeff Leonard, CPP, PSP
Todd P. Letcher
Emblez Longoria, CPP, PSP
Cynthia Long
Richard E. Maier, CPP
Loye A. Manning, CPP, PSP
Robert L. Martin, CPP
Ron Martin, CPP
Roger B. Maslen, CPP
Judith G. Matheny, CPP
Edward F. McDonough, Jr., CPP
Richard A. Michau, CPP
Bonnie S. Michelman, CPP
Owen J. Monaghan, CPP
Wayne Morris, CPP, PSP
Patrick M. Murphy, CPP, PSP
Carla Naude, CPP
James W. Nelson
Robert L. Oatman, CPP
Gerald A. O'Farrell, CPP
Peter E. Ohlhausen
Leonard Ong, CPP
Harm J. Oosten, CPP
S. Steven Oplinger
Denis A. O'Sullivan, CPP
Jaime P. Owens, CPP
Gerard P. Panaro, J.D.
James F. Pastor, Ph.D.
David G. Patterson, CPP, PSP
John T. Perkins, CPP
Karl S. Perman
Kevin E. Peterson, CPP
Charlie R. A. Pierce
Doug Powell, CPP, PSP
Patrick K. Quinn, CPP
Roy A. Rahn, CPP
John D. Rankin, CPP
William G. Rauen, CPP
David L. Ray, LL.B.
Joseph Rector, CPP, PCI, PSP
Ty L. Richmond, CPP
Lisa M. Ruth
Jeffrey J. Ryder, Jr., CPP, PSP
Mark A. Sanna, CPP
Stephen Saravara, III, J.D., CPP
Charles A. Sennewald, CPP
Dennis Shepp, CPP, PCI
Shari Shovlin
Marc Siegel, Ph.D.
Laurie Simmons, CPP, PSP
Dennis Smith, CPP
Stan Stahl, Ph.D.
Paul J. Steiner, Jr., CPP
Pamela M. Stewart, PCI
Dan E. Taylor, Sr., CPP
Lynn A. Thackery, CPP, PSP
Mark L. Theisen, CPP
Dave N. Tyson, CPP
Joann Ugolini, CPP, PSP
Darleen Urbanek
Mike VanDrongelen, CPP, PCI, PSP
Karim Vellani, CPP
Barry J. Walker, CPP
Michael W. Wanik, CPP
Roger D. Warwick, CPP
Fritz Weidner
Richard C. Werth, CPP
Allan R. Wick, CPP, PSP
Anthony S. Wilcox, CPP
Donald S. Williams, CPP
Reginald J. Williams, CPP
Richard F. Williams, CPP
Timothy L. Williams, CPP
Gavin Wilson, PSP
Coleman L. Wolf, CPP
Loftin Woodiel, CPP
Richard P. Wright, CPP
Allison Wylde
Richard Y. Yamamoto, CPP
Scott S. Young, CPP

TABLE OF CONTENTS

PREFACE

CONTRIBUTORS

Chapter 1. **DOGS IN ASSETS PROTECTION** . . . 1

1.1 History . . . 2
1.2 Dog Behavior and Motivation Characteristics . . . 3
1.2.1 Instinctive Drives . . . 3
1.2.2 Senses . . . 3
1.2.3 Intelligence . . . 4
1.2.4 Sensitivity . . . 5
1.2.5 Energy . . . 5
1.2.6 Aggressiveness . . . 6
1.2.7 Willingness . . . 6
1.2.8 Motivation . . . 7
1.3 Care of the Dog . . . 8
1.3.1 Kennels . . . 8
1.3.2 Grooming . . . 9
1.3.3 Inspections . . . 10
1.3.4 Feeding . . . 14
1.3.5 Diseases and Their Prevention . . . 15
1.4 Protection Dog Selection, Training, Deployment, and Cost Advantages . . . 21
1.4.1 Selecting the Dog . . . 21
1.4.2 Training . . . 24
1.4.3 Training Costs . . . 28
1.4.4 Deployment of Protection Dogs . . . 29
1.5 Special Applications and Skill Sets . . . 36
1.5.1 Tracking and Trailing . . . 36
1.5.2 Condition of the Dog for Tracking, Trailing, and Detection Work . . . 38
1.5.3 Detecting Drugs, Explosives, and Accelerants . . . 38
1.5.4 Costs . . . 44
1.6 Legal Liability . . . 45
1.6.1 Criminal Liability . . . 45
1.6.2 Civil Liability . . . 45
1.6.3 Liability Regarding Trespassers . . . 47
1.6.4 Precautions . . . 48
References . . . 50

Chapter 2. **HIGH-RISE STRUCTURES: LIFE SAFETY AND SECURITY CONSIDERATIONS** . . . 51

2.1 Introduction . . . 51
2.1.1 What Is a High-Rise Structure? . . . 51
2.2 Life Safety Considerations . . . 52
2.2.1 Special Concerns of High-Rise Structures . . . 52

2.2.2 Dealing with the Life Safety Problem 56
2.3 Security Considerations 64
2.3.1 Special Concerns of High-Rise Structures 64
2.3.2 Life Safety and Security Dilemma 65
2.3.3 Typical High-Rise 66
2.3.4 Building Operating Modes 67
2.3.5 Building Elements 68
2.3.6 Security Measures 76
2.4 Summary. 86
References/Additional Sources. 87

Chapter 3. **MANAGING CORPORATE SPECIAL EVENTS** 91

3.1 Unique Occasions 92
3.2 Scope of Security Responsibilities 93
3.3 Factors in Event Planning 95
3.3.1 Time-Sensitivity 95
3.3.2 Organizational Structure 95
3.3.3 Volunteers. 95
3.3.4 Location 95
3.3.5 Crowds, Participants, and Attendees. 96
3.3.6 Type of Event 97
3.3.7 Communication 97
3.3.8 Weather 98
3.3.9 Budget 98
3.4 Components of a Special Event Security Plan 99
Appendix A: Model Event Security Plan 102
Additional Reading 109

Chapter 4. **SECURITY IN A GLOBAL ENVIRONMENT** 111

4.1 Policies and Guidelines for International Security Operations 112
4.1.1 Who Should Be Covered? 112
4.1.2 Purpose of the Policies and Guidelines 112
4.2 Accountabilities and Responsibilities 114
4.3 Country Risk Categories 115
4.4 Rating Impact on the Traveler. 117
4.5 Personnel Living Abroad 118
4.6 Risks That May Be Encountered. 119
4.6.1 Crime 119
4.6.2 Arrest and Incarceration. 119
4.6.3 Illness 120
4.6.4 Accident 120
4.6.5 Natural Disaster 120

4.6.6 Geopolitical Events. 120
4.7 Countermeasures 121
4.7.1 General Intelligence Briefings 121
4.7.2 Threat-Specific Briefings 121
4.7.3 Intelligence Forecasts 121
4.7.4 Contingency and Evacuation Planning 121
4.7.5 Communications. 122
4.8 Medical Considerations 123
4.8.1 Medical Assistance Groups 123
4.8.2 Immunizations and Medical History. 124
4.9 Security Awareness Training 125
4.9.1 Embassies and Consulates 126
4.9.2 Culture Orientation 126
4.9.3 Employee Profile and Emergency Information 126
4.9.4 Employee and Asset Tracking. 127
4.9.5 Carrier Safety Analysis 127
4.9.6 Ground Transportation 127
4.9.7 Residence and Hotel Vetting 127
4.9.8 Domestic Help Vetting. 128
4.10 Plant and Office Physical Security 128
4.11 Telecommuting 128
4.12 Supply Chain Due Diligence. 128
4.13 Preemployment Background Checks and Drug Testing 128
4.14 Kidnap/Ransom/Extortion Response 129
4.15 Bribery and Corruption 130
4.16 Information Security 131
Appendix A: Confidential Personal Profile 132
References 137

INDEX. 139

TABLE OF FIGURES

1-1 Average Food Requirements 15
1-2 Items Found to Cause False Alerts in Explosives Detection 41
2-1 High-Rise Office Building General Lobby 66
2-2 Traffic Type and Access 69
2-3 Fresh Air Intake Protection Scheme 75

CHAPTER 1

DOGS IN ASSETS PROTECTION

Dogs have been used effectively in military, law enforcement, and security applications for many years. In planning protection systems, security professionals should consider dogs' unique capabilities as well as their limitations.

Dogs, both wild and domestic, are four-footed carnivores with five non-retractile claws on each front foot and four on each back foot, and they have a constricted head that forms a muzzle. Along with wolves, jackals, and foxes, dogs belong to the family *canidae*. The average life of the domestic dog—*canis familiaris*—is about 12 years, but dogs of some breeds may live 20 years or more if they are very well cared for and provided with life-extending medical care.

The American Kennel Club recognizes more than 150 breeds of dogs, which are classified into eight groups or classes: sporting, hound, working, terrier, toy, non-sporting, herding, and miscellaneous. Security applications typically use dogs from the working and herding groups, though others are also used. What matters most is the overall drive of the individual dog once it has been trained for security work.

Dogs in the working group are bred to perform such jobs as guarding property, pulling rescue sleds, and performing water rescues. Breeds in this group include Akita, Alaskan malamute, Bernese mountain dog, boxer, bull mastiff, Doberman pinscher, Great Dane, Great Pyrenees, greater Swiss mountain dog, komondor, kuvasz, mastiff, Newfoundland, Portuguese water dog, Rottweiler, Saint Bernard, Samoyed, Siberian husky, and standard schnauzer.

Dogs in the herding group share a great ability to control the movement of other animals. Breeds in this group include Australian sheepdog, Australian shepherd, bearded collie, Belgian Malinois, Belgian sheepdog, Belgian Tervuren, border collie, Bouvier des Flandres, Briard, Canaan dog, collie, German shepherd, old English sheepdog, puli, Shetland sheepdog, and Welsh corgi.

1.1 HISTORY

In ancient times, the Greeks and Romans used large, mastiff-type dogs with armor and blade-studded leather collars during warfare to attack and generally disturb enemy lines. After the discovery of gunpowder, dogs were used in military operations primarily as sentries, scouts, and messengers and for guarding prisoners and supplies. During World War II, the U.S. military used about 10,000 dogs. Today, armed forces throughout the world continue to use dogs for many tasks.

The organized use of dogs for law enforcement dates back to at least 1899 when the town of Ghent, Belgium, established a law enforcement training program for dogs. By 1906, police were using 50 to 60 dogs in that city. Around 1910, dogs were used by law enforcement agencies in England and Germany. By 1956, the Baltimore Police Department began an experimental program, pioneering the law enforcement use of dogs in the United States. Dogs are now in regular use in law enforcement agencies around the world.

Common protection functions for which dogs may be trained in private security operations include the following:

- aggressive attack
- building searches
- detection of explosives and incendiary accelerants (substances that boost fires)
- drug detection
- guarding or holding a person in a location
- protection or patrol of areas, with or without handlers
- tracking

1.2 DOG BEHAVIOR AND MOTIVATION CHARACTERISTICS

1.2.1 INSTINCTIVE DRIVES

Two basic drives are prevalent in dogs used for security tasks—the hunt drive and the pack drive. The hunt drive is the impulse of dogs to hunt, chase, and catch prey. It is a basic requirement to make dogs useful to security professionals. This drive must be present to accomplish both detection and protection work. In an untrained dog the drive is usually associated with obtaining food; through training, the drive can be channeled to help the dog pursue and locate other items, such as drugs or lost children. Associated with the hunt drive is the dog's natural predator ability. Dogs can be trained to attack humans without regard to their own safety. Through training, a dog's natural drive is coupled with the desire for a reward.

The pack drive is the propensity for dogs to operate in groups or packs. When domesticated, the dog adopts humans as pack members and defends the pack as well as the territory the pack occupies. The optimal canine is one with equal hunt and pack drives.

1.2.2 SENSES

Humans and dogs have the same basic senses, but some of the dog's senses are much more acute and developed. In security, a dog's senses of smell and hearing are most important, sight and touch less so.

During the imprinting stages of training, a dog must be taught to rely on smell instead of sight. This is especially true when teaching building searches. A dog that has been conditioned to attack a decoy must be retrained and conditioned to find a hidden decoy using the smell of the person. Dogs should be conditioned to use the fastest and easiest means of satisfying their basic needs. For example, if a prey item is a hidden person, the dog learns that by searching for the person by smell rather than by sight, the dog will more quickly obtain the desired reward.

- **Smell.** A dog's ability to detect scents is often described as being more than 100 times greater than that of humans, though the specific degree of difference may not be provable. Regardless, a dog's ability to detect scents is much, much greater than a human's, and some breeds have a truly extraordinary sense of smell.

  Unlike humans, who rely more on sight, dogs work their way through an environment by their sense of smell. To a dog, scent is the primary sense. The powerful sense of smell enables a dog to search for many different objects (including bodies and substances) in both buildings and open spaces, even if the scent is masked. When the air a dog breathes contains odorous particles, the dog begins to sniff, bringing a larger supply of air into the nose and over the areas most richly supplied with the nerves that detect odors.

A dog can detect odors at great distances. For example, a trained dog can sense an intruder's airborne scent more than 250 yards away. Furthermore, dogs can distinguish between odors that seem identical to humans. This ability enables dogs to be trained to recognize and detect a great variety of source materials.

- **Hearing.** A dog's aural acuity far surpasses the human's in both range and pitch. The upper frequency limit of the dog is about twice that of human beings, reaching 30,000 Hz or more. A dog's constant awareness of sounds that are undetected by the human ear is easily observed. The dog's sense of hearing is the principal medium through which the handler communicates with the dog. Some dogs appear to understand the feelings and wishes of their handlers as they are conveyed by voice. Usually a dog can quickly learn to associate the sound and tone of a word with the action expected.
- **Sight.** In general, a dog's vision cannot be compared favorably with that of the normal human. It is widely held that dogs are colorblind and their visual clarity is weak. However, the ability of dogs to detect movement is significant, and the dog will generally be able to successfully alert the handler if there is movement.
- **Touch.** A dog's sensitivity to touch is used primarily during training when the animal is being physically praised or corrected. There is a wide variation among dogs in their responsiveness to the sense of touch. Certain dogs respond to a caress or physical correction, while others appear to be rather insensitive to it. A dog's sensitivity to touch can be determined when it is petted or corrected.

1.2.3 INTELLIGENCE

Dogs are more intelligent than most other animals, except humans and non-human primates. A dog can be trained to respond effectively to a large number of spoken words. A dog's intelligence is gauged in terms of how quickly the dog learns a command, how long it retains the command, and the dog's drive to follow the command. A vocabulary of about 20 words is the norm under usual working conditions; however, some dogs have been trained to respond to as many as 100 oral commands.

A dog may also be deemed highly intelligent if it is unusually capable of learning quickly by experience. Some dogs learn quickly but are difficult to train because they sulk or are stubborn. Some dogs respond only to a handler they like. Individual dogs differ in how much they want to please their pack.

1.2.4 SENSITIVITY

Sensitivity is the type and degree of reaction to a given stimulus. An oversensitive dog can be startled by a stimulus of lower intensity than is required to disturb an under-sensitive dog. The response of the oversensitive dog may be shyness or fright, while the under-sensitive dog might merely turn its head or show no reaction at all. Sensitivities to different stimuli are independent; a dog that cowers when given an oral reprimand may show little response to harsh physical correction. Moreover, trainer characteristics affect a dog's response. A dog may respond to a particular trainer's voice but not his or her touch. In terms of sensitivity, dogs generally fall into three main groups:

- **Oversensitive dogs.** If a dog reacts excessively to a given stimulus, it may be oversensitive. An oversensitive dog will not be able to demonstrate its intelligence in any really usable form. Dogs that are oversensitive to sound, touch, or both are difficult to train and are considered unreliable. They may lie down and shake, as if frightened, when petted. Often these characteristics have to do with events that took place before the dog was acquired for security tasks. In any case, such a dog is unlikely to be useable for assets protection work.
- **Under-sensitive dogs.** A dog that is under-sensitive to both sound and touch is usually difficult to motivate through negative stimuli (correction) or positive stimuli (praise). If the dog is under-sensitive to sound, it may not react to commands given by a handler; if it is under-sensitive to touch, it may not react when petted and may not interpret affection as a reward.
- **Moderately sensitive dogs.** A moderately sensitive dog has normal sensitivity to both sound and touch. With proper training, the dog is likely to willingly respond to hand gestures and vocal commands. The skill with which this type of dog is handled is the deciding factor in how well it will perform. Properly trained, a dog with moderate sensitivity is considered ideal for protection work.

1.2.5 ENERGY

Dogs vary in the amount of energy they demonstrate in their general movements. Some are lazy and move little unless required to, while others are always on the go. A dog between the extremes is generally considered most suitable for protection work. Above-average energy is not particularly necessary or desirable; dogs that possess this trait can usually be trained to control it. A dog with little energy is usually difficult to train.

1.2.6 AGGRESSIVENESS

Aggressiveness should not be confused with energy. An aggressive dog is one that is prone to attack anyone or anything that it perceives as available for attack or that intrudes into its space. In terms of aggressiveness, which is linked to the hunt and pack drives, dogs can be categorized as follows:

- **Over-aggressive dogs.** When an over-aggressive dog sees an agitator, the dog usually becomes greatly excited, lunges at the end of its leash, barks, and continues to bark even after the agitator disappears. Caution must be exercised while working with an over-aggressive dog because it may attempt to bite anyone within reach during a period of excitement. Training must focus on controlling such dogs rather than arousing them. Over-aggressive dogs are difficult to train.
- **Under-aggressive dogs.** A dog that stands still and is indifferent to an agitator is not necessarily under-aggressive. The dog simply may not perceive a threat. A truly under-aggressive dog reacts to an approaching agitator by cowering, hiding behind its handler, or trying to run away. Such dogs are difficult, if not impossible, to train.
- **Moderately aggressive dogs.** Moderately aggressive dogs are the easiest to train and are ideal for assets protection use. On seeing an agitator, the dog becomes alert, shows suspicion of the agitator, and exhibits an eagerness to move toward the agitator.

1.2.7 WILLINGNESS

Willingness refers to a dog's response to commands, its attitude when carrying out duties, and its reaction toward learning new duties. A dog is ranked high in willingness if it continuously responds to a given command in an effort to fulfill it, even though reward or correction cannot be easily perceived as being immediate. Willingness is not the same as intelligence or strength; it is the desire to do the task.

A dog that must constantly be coaxed or admonished is considered an unwilling worker. The unwilling dog may distinguish between work and play. During the play period, the dog may take great pleasure in retrieving, searching for objects, and jumping. However, when training is resumed, the dog may be unwilling to obey commands.

A dog's willingness can be advanced or retarded by the handler. If the handler lacks patience, the dog may work willingly during the first few minutes of a training period but unwillingly during the remainder.

1.2.8 MOTIVATION

Unlike most animals, a dog does not always require tangible rewards or special inducements, such as food, to work or train. Kindness, shown by oral praise or a casual caress, is usually enough to motivate the dog. More than any other form of reward, the dog wants the approval of its handler—probably because of the pack instinct.

A dog has a natural tendency to become attached to and seek companionship from the handler. This attachment grows as the handler feeds, grooms, trains, and works the dog. Through the handler's proper use of dog-training principles, the dog learns to distinguish between praise and correction. A friendly and trusting relationship between the dog and the handler is the motivation needed to train the dog to become highly efficient.

A tangible reward—such as a morsel of food—should not be routinely given after a dog has executed a command properly. Doing so may lead to a dependence on such a reward, and the dog will expect it even when food is not available.

1.3 CARE OF THE DOG

Environment, feeding, and health care are critical factors in maintaining a healthy, effective dog. Inadequate attention to these factors can render an otherwise splendid animal unfit.

1.3.1 KENNELS

Health, comfort, and safety must be considered in planning the location, construction, and maintenance of a kennel. The following criteria are of special importance:

- **Noise.** A dog used for protective activities must be well rested to be alert and efficient while working. A dog continually distracted in the kennel area by outside noise cannot get needed rest, and its performance will therefore be impaired. The kennel facility should not be located in an area where the average sound level for a 24-hour period exceeds 75 decibels. Kennels should be at least 150 to 200 yards (137 to 183 meters) from residential or commercial areas to minimize distracting noises. To further reduce noise and other distractions, natural barriers—such as hills, trees, and large shrubs—should be put between built-up areas and the kennel. Artificial barriers may be needed while shrubs grow to the proper height and density or when no natural barriers are available.
- **Drainage.** Kennels should be constructed above ground level on a raised platform and situated on gently sloping ground to eliminate any possibility of standing water in the area. To reduce cross-contamination, the drainage system should be designed so each kennel run drains independently.
- **Water supply.** An adequate supply is needed for cleaning and drinking purposes. Since impure water is a source of disease for both dogs and handlers, the water supply should be approved for human consumption. Also, an adequate water supply must be available for fire protection.
- **Fire protection.** Water-type fire extinguishers (Class A rating) are generally used in the kennel area, with one extinguisher provided for each 2,500 square feet (232 square meters) of floor space in the kennel and support facilities.[1] Requirements should be reviewed with the local fire department. Access to the kennel site by fire department vehicles should be considered in selecting a location. Automatic sprinklers using clean water are also appropriate. Chemical systems can be as toxic for dogs as for humans.
- **Lighting, ventilation, and heat.** Adequate lighting is needed for nighttime operation and for safety. Roof ventilators that can be opened and closed may also be provided. All other exterior openings should be designed so they can be closed. Electric heating cables can be embedded in concrete to provide heat during cold weather. Ideal

[1] In the United States, in accordance with National Fire Protection Association Standard #10 for Portable Fire Extinguishers, the largest area within a light hazard occupancy to be protected by a single portable extinguisher would be 6,000 square feet (557 square meters) and the smallest permissible extinguisher would be 2A.

temperature varies among breeds, but generally the kennel should be within the range of 60 to 75 degrees Fahrenheit (15.5 to 23.9 degrees Celsius) with a relative humidity of about 40 percent.

- **Areas relating to kennels.** Outside dog runs are usually necessary. A chain link fence 8 feet (2.4 meters) high surrounding the kennels is adequate to keep most dogs contained. However, dogs that can climb fences require a closed fence cage. Signs instructing unauthorized individuals not to enter the area should be posted on the perimeter fence.
- **Sanitation.** The kennels should be maintained in a sanitary condition. They all should be thoroughly cleaned every day. Additionally, kennels should be disinfected periodically in accordance with the instructions of a veterinarian. Dropping are a common source of infection and should be removed from the runs as often as required and always before runs are washed down to avoid contaminating other areas. The method for disposing of droppings depends on local conditions and the type of sewage system. If removed in cans, the cans should be cleaned and disinfected after each use. Also, refuse and garbage should not be allowed to accumulate as it may attract rats and insects. In regions where mosquitoes are a problem, control measures must be taken around any ditches and swampy areas near the kennels.
- **Maintenance.** Proper preventive maintenance of the kennel results in easier and less expensive upkeep. The handlers should inspect each dog's kennel every day. Loose or worn hinges on the door or gate should be repaired or replaced, and the sides of the kennel and water container should be inspected.
- **Feeding area.** The food preparation area must be kept clean. Food and water vessels should be cleaned daily, and any utensils used to prepare food should be cleaned immediately after use. If canned foods are used, can openers must be kept clean. Dry food should be stored in rodent-proof containers and inspected for contamination before being fed to the dogs.

1.3.2 GROOMING

Grooming has a twofold purpose. It is essential for the care of the dog, and it aids in bonding the dog and the handler. Thorough grooming is necessary for the dog's skin and hair and should be done routinely, preferably daily. The dog should first be given a brisk rubdown, with the fingertips moving *against the grain* of the hair. This loosens any dead skin, hair, or dirt and brings it to the surface. It also massages the skin. Next the handler should provide a thorough but gentle brushing *against the grain* to remove the loosened skin, hair, and dirt. The handler should follow up by brushing the coat *with the grain*. The last step is to rub the coat with the palms of the hands *with the grain* of the hair. This step helps distribute the natural oil and gives the coat a glossy appearance. Occasionally, the dog's coat should be combed and examined for ticks, burrs, cuts, abrasions, and lumps.

Bathing is not a part of routine grooming, but a bath may be necessary occasionally. A dog's skin has many glands that produce an oily substance that keeps the skin soft and repels water. Excessive bathing may lead to dryness of the skin, resulting in a variety of skin ailments. The handler should ask a veterinarian about proper bathing frequency, type of soap, and protection for the dog's eyes and ears. A thorough rinsing after the bath is important because if soap is left in the coat, it becomes sticky, collects dirt, and may cause skin irritation. After the dog has been thoroughly towel-dried, in warm weather it may be gently exercised in the sun to complete the drying. A dog should not be bathed in cold or wet weather unless it can remain in a warm place until completely dry.

1.3.3 INSPECTIONS

During regular grooming, every part of the dog's anatomy should be checked for indications of illness or injury. Over time, the handler will gain a sense of what the dog should look like and how it should act when it is healthy. The handler knows what is normal for a particular dog, how the coat looks, how many bowel movements the dog has each day, and how much the dog routinely eats. For example, the handler should be able to discern that the animal did not eat all its food for a day or two, that it is experiencing hair loss and reddened skin on some area of its body, or that a discharge is coming from the dog's nose.

When a handler notices anything abnormal about the appearance or actions of the dog, he or she could contact a veterinarian immediately. Early detection of an illness or injury improves the chance of recovery, and uninformed treatment may do more harm than good. The following are the major elements of inspection:

Eyes

Care must be taken not to injure the dog's eyes when examining them. Illnesses of the body are frequently accompanied by changes in the eyes, and many illnesses affect only the eyes. Normally, a dog's eyes are bright and clear, while the surrounding membranes have a healthy pink color. Symptoms of abnormality include the following:

- reddish or yellowish discoloration of the membranes and whites of the eyes
- paleness of the eye membranes
- whitish or yellowish discharges from the eyes
- cloudiness or other discoloration of the clear portion of the eyes
- puffiness of the eyelids
- partial or complete closure of the eyelids
- membranes covering more of the cornea than is normal

Ears

The erect external portion of the ear is called the ear flap. Leading downward from the base of the ear flap is the ear canal. The portion of the canal that can be seen with the naked eye is known as the vertical canal; the deeper portion, which cannot be seen, is the horizontal canal. Small quantities of brownish wax are frequently seen in the vertical canal, and this is normal. To rule out problems, the ears should be checked by the veterinarian even when they appear to need only cleaning. The handler should not probe into the ear canal with any object. A veterinarian should be informed of any of the following symptoms of abnormality in the ears:

- reddish discoloration, swelling, or large amount of discharge in the ear canal
- foul odor coming from the canals
- shaking of the head
- holding the ear flap down
- holding the head to one side
- twitching the ear
- scratching or pawing at the ear
- evidence of pain when the ear is touched

Nose

The handler should not probe into the dog's nose with any object. The black pad at the end of the dog's nose is usually shiny and moist. A persistently dry and dull nose may be a symptom of illness. Other symptoms of abnormality include the following:

- watery, yellowish, or red-tinged discharge
- sneezing, snorting, and pawing at the nose

Mouth

Normally, the gums and inner aspect of the lips are a healthy pink, while the teeth are firm and shiny white in color. Loose and broken teeth, tartar accumulations, and foreign objects lodged between the teeth require the attention of a veterinarian. Handlers should remember that dogs require periodic dental attention to prevent tooth loss and periodontal disease. Symptoms of illness include the following:

- paleness of the gums
- sores
- persistent drooling
- bloody saliva
- foul breath
- gagging or pawing at the mouth

Feet

Proper care of the feet is essential if a dog is to perform effectively. The feet should be checked for foreign objects that may be caught in the pads as well as for cuts, bruises, or abrasions of the pads.

In cold weather, long-haired dogs should have their paw-hair clipped to ease snow removal and cleaning. Rock salt and other chemicals can be irritating to the pads of the paws. If the dog works in areas where ice melting compounds are used, the paws should be thoroughly rinsed and dried after contact to avoid irritation.

Dogs usually keep their nails at the proper length so the tips of the nails do not touch the ground when they stand. Sometimes, however, the nails become so long that they interfere with the dog's work. Any overly long, broken, or split nails must be given attention. Handlers should not neglect the nails on the dewclaws—the innermost claws—since they are not worn down by contact with the ground and may grow until they curve back into the dog's leg.

Skin and Hair

If the dog is well fed and groomed, the dog's coat will have a glossy appearance and the skin will be soft and pliable. The coat is subject to changes in appearance when the climate and season change, experiencing shedding in warm weather and thickening in cold weather. The coat should always be checked for fleas, ticks, and lice. Indications of skin abnormality include the following:

- reddening
- scabbing
- persistent scratching
- shedding that is abnormal for the season or climate
- loss of hair in one or more spots
- dryness
- loss of pliability

Limbs

A dog's legs must also be inspected for wounds, swelling, and sores. On the forelegs, there is normally an area on the outer side of each elbow known as the callus. This is an area of hairless, thickened skin about an inch in diameter. If the callus becomes inflamed, a veterinarian should treat it.

Genitals

In a male dog, the penis is subject to a variety of injuries. A veterinarian should be called to inspect any discharge from the penis or its sheath, bleeding from the prepuce, or swelling, reddening, or scabbing of the scrotum. In a female dog there is normally no discharge from the external opening of the genital tract. A veterinarian should consulted if there is reddening of the vulva or of the skin in that area or a discharge from the vulva.

Anal region

On either side of the rectum near the anus is a small sac known as the anal sac. These sacs are a frequent source of trouble. The handler should look for any swelling and reddening of the skin in this area or of the anus itself. When the anal sacs need to be emptied or are infected, the dog may turn to bite at the area or may slide along the ground while in a sitting position. This indicates a problem that requires the attention of a veterinarian.

Temperature

A dog's body temperature is determined rectally and is one of the best indications of its health. Normally, the body temperature is within 101 to 102 degrees Fahrenheit (38.3 to 38.9 degrees Celsius). Variations from this range frequently indicate an illness. However, some variation in temperature may not be abnormal following exercise or agitation. A veterinarian should be consulted when unexpected variations occur or when variations are larger than usual.

Body functions

Disturbances to breathing and digestion are accompanied by many symptoms, such as lethargy in a normally active dog or hostility in a normally friendly one. The handler should be alert to such conditions.

Any change in appetite, thirst, or any change in the manner of breathing—such as an unusual amount of panting—should be noted. Vomiting may occur, or there may be a change in the nature of the intestinal contents as evidenced by a very soft or watery stool. Blood may be seen in the vomitus or in the stool. By observing the dog during urination or defecation, it is possible to detect blood in the urine or determine whether the dog is having difficulty passing urine or stools. If there is blood in the urine, the handler should take note of whether it is in the first or last portion or distributed throughout. The handler should pay attention to the frequency of urination and defecation and should note any increase or decrease in the frequency.

Attitude

One of the best indications of a dog's health is its attitude. The handler can usually detect an attitude change. If a dog begins to be unduly nervous, shows a loss of vitality and energy, or displays an increased desire for sleep or is inattentive, the dog's physical condition should be evaluated.

1.3.4 FEEDING

For good health, a dog must be fed a proper diet, which includes an adequate number of calories. The calories required will depend on the dog's weight and activity as well as the climatic conditions under which the dog must work.

Dogs are carnivorous, but they require more than just meat in their diet; they also need vegetables and cereals. Like humans, dogs need carbohydrates, fats, proteins, vitamins, and minerals. A dog requires 36 nutrients to remain in good health (National Research Council, 1985, p. 44).

Formerly, dogs were fed table scraps or whatever food was plentiful in the region where they lived, but a diet lacking nutritional balances will make a dog sick. Pet food manufacturers now produce appealing dog food that is also nutritionally complete. Dry and soft dog foods typically have similar nutritional value. That value can be determined by reading the label. In the United States, if the label indicates the food is "balanced" or "complete," it meets or exceeds the standards established by the American Association of Feed Control Officials (AAFCO). AAFCO is an association of government regulatory officials and manufacturers' representatives that provides a forum for the development of standards and laws for animal feed. AAFCO conducts an analytical sampling program to help laboratories maintain accurate analyses of feeds.

Manufacturers in the United States are not required to list the 36 ingredients specified by the National Research Council on the label. However, they are required by federal and state regulations to list on the label the ingredients actually in the container. The required nutrients can be obtained from many sources. Protein, for example, may be obtained from soybean meal, yeast, fish, or cottage cheese, while grains, such as corn or rice, may be used to provide carbohydrates.

Vitamin and mineral supplements may also be necessary in a dog's diet. If good health and performance are expected, a dog must be fed the correct amount of each of the required nutrients. If anything is added, like table scraps, the intricate, interrelated balance of nutrients may be upset and the health of the dog may be adversely influenced. Usually, a good commercially prepared dog food is adequate. If supplements are used, a veterinarian should prescribe them. An adequate supply of clean water should always be provided with the food.

The amount of food a dog should be fed can be gauged by observing the amount the dog will eat with gusto. In cold weather, a dog that spends considerable time outdoors, or a working dog, needs additional calories to regulate the body temperature. As a general rule, dogs of a given weight should be fed at the following rates:

Weight of Dog	Average Daily Food Requirement
150 lb (68 kg)	5.25 lb (2.4 kg)
100 lb (45 kg)	4 lb (1.8 kg)
75 lb (34 kg)	3.25 lb (1.5 kg)
50 lb (23 kg)	2.5 lb (1.1 kg)

Figure 1-1
Average Food Requirements

Dogs should be fed at the same time once a day, usually at the end of their workday. Each dog should be fed from its own pan, which should be removed and cleaned after the dog has finished eating. The food should not be left out longer than 20 or 30 minutes. If the dog does not eat the food within that period, it should be taken away. Doing so teaches the dog to eat when the food is set out.

A dog should also be trained to refuse food from strangers and not to eat food it might find because of the possibility that it might contain poison. Dog training requires an expert, and the specialized training of refusing food from strangers should be included as an item taught by the dog trainer.

1.3.5 DISEASES AND THEIR PREVENTION

The following are some of the more common diseases that might affect a dog's performance. Many of the diseases can be prevented through immunization.

Contagious Diseases

These diseases are caused by a microscopic organism—such as a virus or bacterium—transmitted between animals (including humans). Below are the more common contagious diseases that affect dogs:

- **Canine distemper.** A widespread, highly contagious, and usually fatal viral disease, canine distemper occurs primarily in young dogs or in older dogs that have not been immunized against the disease. The virus is airborne and easily transmitted from dog to dog. This disease does not affect humans. Lethargy, dry nose, and lack of appetite are among the early symptoms.

- **Infectious canine hepatitis.** Infectious canine hepatitis, a viral disease, is seen most commonly in young dogs but may affect older dogs that have not been immunized. The mortality rate from hepatitis is not as high as it is from canine distemper, but recovery is usually slow. The virus is spread through the urine of infected animals. It may be spread from one animal to another by the use of common feeding and drinking utensils that have been contaminated by urine. The canine hepatitis virus does not cause hepatitis in humans.
- **Leptospirosis.** Known commonly as "lepto," this disease is caused by a spiral-shaped bacterium called a spirochete and is fairly common in dogs. The disease can also infect animals other than dogs and can be transmitted to a human. Lepto is spread through the urine of infected animals, most commonly dogs and rats. Dogs' food and water must be kept uncontaminated. Rodent control is important in preventing the spread of this disease. If lepto is known or suspected to exist in an area, dogs should not be allowed to enter streams, rivers, or other bodies of water unnecessarily, since the water may be contaminated by the urine of the infected animals. Also, because of the possibility of human infection with lepto, those handling dogs must practice sound personal hygiene at all times.

A dog infected with any of the preceding three diseases—distemper, hepatitis, or leptospirosis—usually exhibits one or more of the following symptoms: elevated temperature, loss of appetite, depression, loss of weight, loss of energy, diarrhea, vomiting, coughing, thick discharge from the eyes and nose, muscle stiffness, or convulsions. When a dog exhibits any of these symptoms or other changes in normal body functions, a veterinarian must be notified.

- **Rabies.** Like lepto, rabies (hydrophobia) can be transmitted to humans. The rabies virus in the saliva of infected animals is transmitted to people through bite wounds. Rabies affects the central nervous system of warm-blooded animals and is fatal if untreated. Death almost always occurs within 10 days after an animal has started showing signs of the disease. Signs may first appear in humans three to six weeks after a bite by an infected animal. In the United States, some of the animals most frequently affected are skunks, raccoons, bats, foxes, dogs, coyotes, cattle, and cats.

  Symptoms of rabies in dogs may include a sudden change in temperament or attitude, indiscriminate snapping and biting, excitement, difficulty in swallowing water or food, blank expression, slack jaw, excessive drooling from the mouth, paralysis, coma, and ultimately death. Rabid wild animals often lose their fear of humans and domestic animals.
- **Lyme disease.** Lyme disease is an infectious disease syndrome spread primarily by a tick as small as the period at the end of this sentence. It is caused by a spirochete that is

transmitted to animals and humans by the bite of the tick. In people, the disease can appear to be as simple as the flu or as serious as Alzheimer's disease. If untreated, it can lead to joint damage and heart and neurological complications. In animals, the disease can mimic flu-like symptoms of chronic arthritis and lead to joint damage, heart complications, and kidney problems.

In the United States, Lyme disease has been reported in 45 states; however, the disease is mainly clustered in the mid-Atlantic, Northeast, North Central, and Pacific coastal regions. The greatest chance of infection through the bite of a tick occurs from May through September. There is a moderate risk in fall and a low risk during winter. It is important to remember that not all ticks carry Lyme disease. A tick bite does not necessarily mean the disease will follow, and prompt removal of the tick lessens the chance of disease transmission. (The proper procedure for removing a tick is discussed under "External Parasites" below.)

Vaccines are available to protect against Lyme disease in dogs and humans. A veterinarian should be consulted concerning the threat of Lyme disease in the area in which the dog is housed and worked.

- **Other diseases.** Some contagious animal diseases for which vaccines are not available are upper respiratory infections, pneumonia, and gastroenteritis. Dogs infected with these diseases may show symptoms similar to animals infected with canine distemper, infectious canine hepatitis, or leptospirosis. Symptoms include elevated temperature, loss of appetite, loss of energy, vomiting, diarrhea, and coughing.

Parasitic Diseases

Dogs may also be affected by parasitic infections. Animal parasites infest another species of animal—called the host—to feed from the host's body. Most parasites that use the dog as a host are detrimental to its health. Also, some parasites of the dog can spread harmful, disease-producing organisms to humans. They are not always discernible to the unpracticed eye and can be sometimes present in great numbers before the dog exhibits symptoms of their presence. Symptoms of infestation include frequent scratching, bald spots, or inflammation of the skin.

External Parasites

External parasites cause damage by sucking blood from the skin or actually eating the skin tissue. The dog then bites and scratches the irritated areas, which may lead to severe skin infections and drastically affect the dog's working ability. The external parasites that most commonly affect dogs are ticks, fleas, lice, and mites.

- **Ticks.** These are small parasites common in many parts of the world. They suck blood from the dog, leading to a serious loss of blood. Ticks are most often observed motionless with their heads buried deep in the dog's skin. Ticks are capable of spreading a variety of diseases by sucking blood or tissue fluid from a diseased animal and then moving to another animal and burrowing into the skin.

Tick removal requires caution because ticks carry diseases that can infect humans and because the dog's skin may become inflamed if the tick is not removed completely. In removing a tick, the fingers or a pair of tweezers should be used on the tick as close to the skin as possible. The tick's head should be withdrawn from the skin by slow, gentle traction.

Ticks deep in the ear canals must be removed only by a veterinarian. After removal, ticks should be disposed of by immersion in alcohol followed by a flushing down the nearest drain. Personnel should always wash their hands after handling ticks. It may be useful in cases of serious tick bite situations to preserve the dead ticks for inspection by the vet.

When not on dogs, ticks can be found in cracks in the floors, on the sides of the kennel, or in grass or bushes. Ticks may live away from the dog's body as long as a year. Control, therefore, requires treating the kennels and surrounding areas with insecticides. The use of insecticides should be approved by a veterinarian first.

- **Fleas.** These irritate the skin of a dog and spread disease. They crawl or hop through the hair of a dog's coat. They may also transfer to a human host. They sometimes live in cracks in the kennel or in the grass. They are a primary cause of the transmission of tapeworm among dogs. To control fleas, it is necessary to ensure that the kennel is kept sanitary and that the dog and surrounding areas of the kennel are properly treated. Infested dogs may require complete immersion in a special solution to remove the fleas.
- **Lice.** These also irritate a dog's skin. Biting lice live off the dog's tissues, and sucking lice suck blood. Extensive blood sucking can cause anemia and greatly weaken the dog. Lice are so small that they frequently escape notice. Often dogs with just a few lice develop severe itching while those harboring thousands of lice may not scratch themselves at all. Biting lice are usually immobile and stand perpendicular to the skin. The females lay eggs that hatch and develop into adult lice in just three weeks. Lice eggs (nits) and are small white or gray crescent-shaped objects fastened to the hairs. Lice can live only a short time when they are not on the dog's body.
- **Ear mites.** These live in the ear canals and cause a severe irritation. Affected dogs not only scratch at the ears but also cock their head to one side. The ear canals usually contain a large amount of dark-colored waxy discharge when mites are present. Ear mites are small but are visible to the naked eye as tiny, white crawling specks.

  Mites that live in the animal's skin are known as mange mites. Two types of mange are common and may be present at any time of the year. Demodectic mange or red mange is common in short-haired animals and is marked in the early stages by small areas of hair loss and a red, irritated appearance. Sarcoptic mange or scabies is marked by severe itching, irritation, and loss of hair. This type of mange can be transmitted to humans and other dogs by direct contact. Anyone handling affected dogs must practice good personal hygiene. Both types of mange are serious skin diseases that can develop into severe skin infections. Mange mites are too small to be seen with the naked eye and can only be seen by taking a skin scraping of the infested area and observing it under a microscope. Mites, like lice, spend their entire life on the dog.

Internal Parasites

Internal parasites live in the body of a dog and cause damage by irritating the tissues, constantly robbing the body of blood, stealing essential nutrients, or interfering with a specific body action. Only a part of the life cycle of the internal parasites discussed here is spent in the body.

- **Hookworms.** These parasites, which live in a dog's intestines, are among the most harmful internal parasites. They are small and threadlike, only one-half to three-quarters of an inch in length (13 mm to 19 mm). They suck blood and also cause blood loss by grasping and tearing at the intestinal wall with the many hooks in their mouths. The female hookworms produce eggs that are passed in the infected dog's stools. Immature hookworm larvae develop from these eggs. The larvae can then infect the same or another dog. The larvae gain entrance to the body by penetrating the dog's skin or by being swallowed as the dog licks the ground or the skin. After the larvae enter into the body they pass directly to the intestine or travel through the body tissues to the lungs. Those reaching the lungs are coughed up and swallowed, then reach the intestine. Once they are in the intestine, they develop into adult hookworms, and the life cycle begins again.

  Dogs infected with hookworms may have a variety of symptoms. Membranes of the mouth and eyes may be pale, stools may be loose and bloody, or the animal may lose weight. A veterinarian must examine an infected dog's stool by microscope to find hookworm eggs. Control of hookworms can generally be accomplished by giving dogs a chemical which interrupts the life cycle of the worms.

- **Roundworms.** These parasites also live in the intestine. They are larger than hookworms, varying from 2 to 8 inches in length (51 mm to 203 mm). The life cycle is similar to that of the hookworm, but the eggs do not develop into larvae until a dog has swallowed them. Adult roundworms cause trouble by robbing the infected animal of essential nutrients, while the larvae produce an irritation as they travel through the lungs. Symptoms of an infected animal may include vomiting, diarrhea, loss of weight, or coughing. Diagnosis is made by finding the eggs in the stool. Occasionally, adult worms may be vomited or passed in a stool, in which case they may be seen. Control measures involve treating the animals and ensuring good sanitary practices in the kennel area.

- **Whipworms.** These intestinal parasites are smaller than roundworms but larger than hookworms. The life cycle is very similar to that of the roundworm, but the larvae do not travel to the lungs before becoming adults in the intestine of the infected animal. Symptoms of infection may include diarrhea, loss of weight, or paleness of the membranes of the mouth and eyes. The microscopic eggs are found in the stool. This type of parasite can be controlled by treating the individual animal and keeping the kennel area sanitary.

- **Tapeworms.** These parasites have many segments and a head. They are long, flat, and ribbon-like in appearance, and they use their heads to attach themselves to the wall of the intestine. The life cycle of the tapeworm is complex. After the eggs have been passed in the dog's stool, they are eaten by the larvae of the dog flea. The larvae of the tapeworm develop in the flea and when a dog eats the adult flea, the tapeworm larvae gain entrance to the dog's intestine where they develop into adult tapeworms.

  The symptoms produced by tapeworms may not be noticeable except for diarrhea, loss of appetite, or loss of weight. Some tapeworms pass through the bodies of rabbits, mice, or squirrels, during their life cycle. Dogs become infected by eating an animal that contains tapeworm larvae. The eggs of the tapeworm may not be detected during stool examinations; however, segments may be seen in the stool or among the hairs in the dogs' anal region. They are small, white objects about one-fourth of an inch long (6 mm), and they may be moving in a rhythmic manner. Control measures include treatment of the infected animal, good sanitation in the kennel area, control of fleas, and preventing the dog from eating infected animals.

- **Heartworms.** These are found not in the intestine but in the heart and lungs. Heartworms interfere with a dog's heart action and circulation. Adult worms in the heart produce larvae called microfilaria. The microfilaria circulate in the infected animal's bloodstream where they may be picked up by mosquitoes, which spread the heartworm parasite from one dog to another. The larvae continue their development in the mosquito and then are injected back into the same or another dog's tissue when the mosquito feeds. The microfilaria gradually travel to the heart of the dog and develop into adults, where the life cycle begins again. Dogs infected with heartworms may exhibit coughing, loss of weight, breathing difficulty, or a quick loss of energy. The disease is diagnosed by the veterinarian when microfilaria are discovered during a blood test. Treatment is then given to kill the adult worms and the microfilaria. In addition, chemicals may be used to interrupt the life cycle of the worms. Mosquitoes should be controlled as well.

Noninfectious Diseases

Many diseases that affect dogs are not caused by viruses, bacteria, or other infectious agents. Some of these are arthritis, bloating, chronic kidney disease, and allergies. Some symptoms of a noninfectious disease may resemble those of an infectious disease. Other symptoms are hardly noticeable and may include gradual loss of weight, excessive water consumption, excessive urination, or obscure lameness. Any abnormal changes in a dog's health or activities should be reported to a veterinarian.

1.4 PROTECTION DOG SELECTION, TRAINING, DEPLOYMENT, AND COST ADVANTAGES

This section examines the following:

- evaluation and selection of a dog for assets protection and security-related tasks
- training of dogs for such work
- use of dogs in area protection, alone or with a handler
- cost advantages of the use of dogs in security

To be effective, a dog selection and training program must address the specific protection tasks to be performed. The usual assets protection tasks for which dogs are selected and trained include these:

- protection of an area with a handler
- protection or patrol of an area alone, without a handler
- guarding or holding a person in a location
- aggressive attack
- tracking
- detection of drugs, explosives, accelerants, and other substances

Because of the restrictions on time and the effort needed to keep skills at the optimal level, generally a dog should be trained specifically for protection or detection, not both. Detection dogs need constant retraining.

1.4.1 SELECTING THE DOG

In general, any kind of dog can qualify for protection work. The animal, however, should have the size, intelligence, courage, vitality, strength, and other necessary characteristics to perform its function. The dog can be any color, should be bold but not ferocious, and should respond well to training at about 12 months of age. Usually only male dogs are used, although females may be acceptable if they are spayed. The German shepherd and the Doberman pinscher are the most popular breeds used for protection tasks in the United States. The German shepherd (correctly bred—not inbred) is probably the better breed. In other parts of the world, indigenous breeds are also successfully used for protection-related tasks.

General Criteria

- **Background.** A dog considered for protection tasks does not need to be a purebred or show quality but, at the same time, should not be selected from an animal shelter. Generally, a shelter cannot determine a dog's past. Poor inherited traits can cause temperamental, emotional, physical, or mental problems. The dog's prior environment may have harmed its instinct for territorial protection.

  Selecting a dog from a professional breeder is usually best—if the professional's reputation is credible and can be verified. A reputable breeder will normally replace the dog or otherwise make an adjustment if the dog selected proves unhealthy or physically incapable of performing. The breeder usually gives a written assurance against physical problems. A dog who has lived with the breeder for a year or longer is unlikely to have had sufficient contact with humans and usually is not a good candidate for training. Such a dog may also suffer from ailments like kennel blindness and should be carefully examined by a veterinarian.

- **Physical characteristics.** The dog should be at least middle-sized as defined by international competition standards. Proportion should be harmonious; the dog should have a straight, solid back and shoulders. The hindquarters must be strong, and all the animal's teeth should be present and healthy. A dog's shyness can be determined by observing its behavior and approach to strangers. Another test of shyness is to fire a blank pistol from about 30 ft. (9 m) behind the dog. A trained handler can estimate timidity from the dog's reaction. The mere presence of shyness in a dog is usually enough to question its value for protection work. A veterinarian should examine the dog, and X-rays should be taken to evaluate the skeletal structure. A male dog should be examined to determine that it is not a monorchid—an animal having only one descended testicle. Monorchids tend to be temperamental and may also be negatively affected physically by the condition.

- **Temperament.** An acceptable dog has an even temperament. It can be reserved and cautious in a quiet environment but also has a strong desire to play and be active. The dog may appear alert and cautious when people approach, but it must not display unwarranted aggression. The acceptable dog is inquisitive and inclined to investigate sounds and objects.

- **Courage.** Courage is the lack of fear in a threatening environment. The acceptable dog stands its ground in the face of a threat. The dog should not show unwarranted aggression but should not stand totally passive—and must never retreat. When the threat is no longer present, the dog should return to its normal state but remain alert and vigilant for a period. The age, previous training, and maturity of the dog should be considered when conducting a test of courage. The objective of a courage test is not to force the dog into submission but to determine the point at which courage appears and the point at which it begins to diminish.

- **Hardness.** Hardness is the willingness of the dog to overcome undesirable forces to accomplish a goal. One test for an untrained dog is to toss a ball or favorite toy into a corner of a room in which many chairs and tables are stacked haphazardly. A hard dog will climb into and around the objects with little apprehension to get the ball.

After meeting the selection criteria, the dog should be placed on probation for a two-week training period so that its ability to respond can be closely observed. The suitability of the dog can usually be determined during this time. However, even after the initial period, the dog may exhibit traits that make it unsuitable for protection work. If so, it should be dropped from the training program immediately.

German Shepherd

The German shepherd is known throughout the world for uncanny intelligence and faithfulness. The German shepherd is the most popular dog for police and protection work in the United States. To some degree, this breed resembles its ancestor, the wolf. It is characterized by power, agility, balance, and coordination. The German shepherd male in use in the United States stands about 28 inches or more at the shoulder, although the American Kennel Club Standards specify that the male should stand 24 to 26 inches in height. Ideally, the German shepherd weighs between 75 and 90 pounds; has a clean-cut head, powerful jaws, and 42 teeth; erect, moderately pointed ears; a straight outer coat and protective woolly inner coat; and a long bushy tail that hangs at a slight curve when the animal is at rest. The nose should be black; eyes should be dark and almond-shaped. The color of the dog's coat varies in shades and mixtures of black and brown.

This dog is very popular because it responds well to training, has a keen sense of smell, and usually has the ability to respond to commands. This type is a very strong animal. Its jaws can exert 500–600 lb. of pressure per square inch (35–42 kgf/cm^2) and can easily break a man's arm.

Known in Great Britain as the Alsatian, the German shepherd originated in Western Europe and was introduced into the United States in 1904. The modern German shepherd was developed by Rittmeister von Stephanitz, who selected three herding dogs and by careful, selective breeding developed the present breed.

Not every German shepherd can be a good protection dog. Indiscriminate breeding practices over the years have caused a steady decline in the temperament and trainability of the breed. As a result, there seem to be as many bad German shepherds as good. Some are shy, others overly aggressive. Dog handlers often state that only one German shepherd in 10 has the necessary qualifications for protection work. However, the numbers are more favorable if breeding programs used in Germany or by the United States military are followed. These rigorous breeding programs are subject to high requirements and selectivity. German training programs are now followed in some parts of the United States. Many professional breeders see trainability and character as essential criteria for their breeding programs.

Doberman Pinscher

The pinscher originated about 1890 in Thuringen, Germany and was bred from a mixture of German shepherd, Rottweiler, black and tan terrier, and German pinscher. Over the years this animal has been carefully and selectively bred to create a fighter and an excellent dog for protection purposes. Louis Dobermann, from whom the species takes its name, developed the breed. It became popular in the United States about 1921. This dog is large, compactly built, muscular, and powerful, with great endurance and speed.

It is energetic, alert, and fearless. It learns quickly and will attack anything without any apparent care for its own safety. The male should be 25–28 in. (64–71 cm) from ground to shoulders, the female 24–26 in. (61–66 cm). The coat is short, and colors are normally black, red, blue, and fawn. Black dogs usually have rust markings above the eyes and on the muzzle, throat, fore chest, and feet and also below the tail. The head is wedge-shaped. In the United States, the ears are normally cropped. The tail is usually cut at the second joint shortly after the puppy is born.

1.4.2 TRAINING

Only a qualified professional should undertake the training of a protection dog. Qualified trainers, available in most localities, can either provide already-trained animals or train those supplied by the user. Training is a complex task that involves specific techniques and methods. Understanding the strengths and limitations of training provides an appreciation for the use of dogs in protection work and some insights into how to handle the dogs effectively after they have been trained.

Training Methods

Professional dog trainers use a variety of methods, as not all dogs respond to the same methods. The trainer should understand animal behavior well and be able to study the behavior of any specific dog. The strengths and weaknesses in the dog's drives are paramount in determining which training methods to use. Usually, several methods are used with a single dog.

The most common methods are as follows:

- positive reinforcement (praise) tailored to the dog's specific predominant drives
- compulsion (negative corrections) through the handler's voice or with equipment such as a shock collar
- inducement (balls, toys, companionship, or food)

The training course for a dog who will be used with a handler (a dog team) might include the following topics:

- obedience or controllability
- agility (confidence course)
- article search
- box search or suspect search in a building
- basic tracking and scouting
- bite work in prey and defense
- criminal apprehension, protection, and control
- tactical deployment

The dog can usually learn more rapidly if an exercise is structured so the dog can complete the task while in a specific drive that is natural to the particular dog. For example, in early agility or confidence training, inducement in the form of a ball or other reward might be used to encourage the dog to surmount an obstacle. A particular dog may require that the reward be given after every jump. When the dog is conditioned to the desired behavior, the use of inducement should be reduced and compulsion used to complete the training for the task. The successful trainer avoids anthropomorphism (attributing human characteristics to animals) and focuses on dog behavior. Most successful trainers seem to like dogs but avoid becoming overly attached to any particular dog.

Training Limitations

Dogs do not understand the actual meanings of words but associate the sound of a word with the movement or action required. Dogs are unable to reason as humans or non-human primates can, and they are believed to have no abstract notions of orders, obedience, duty, guilt, blame, punishment, morality, or good and evil. Dogs can be trained because their natural drives are stimulated during training.

A dog's pack drive motivates it to remain in close contact with associates. While the dog lives with humans, that instinct influences the dog to remain close to humans and to depend on them for leadership. The result is that a dog can be trained to protect humans in the same way it would protect other members of the pack. Further, there is a natural instinct to acknowledge rank within the pack. The leader of a pack of wild dogs has absolute power, and all members of the pack are subordinate to it.

In training a dog, a human takes the place of the pack leader. Consequently, the dog subordinates itself to the human leader if treated as it would be by a canine pack leader. However, the instinct for subordination is generally not enough to guarantee that a dog will act effectively to protect humans or their property. The dog must learn to respond in the required way.

A dog also has drives that are likely to interfere with protection work. These must be controlled through training. For example, an untrained dog walking with its master in a field may chase a rabbit because of a natural chase instinct. This instinct is likely to be significantly stronger than any influence the human might attempt to exert. After the chase, the dog normally returns to the master and shows great pleasure in being reunited. To control such behavior, the dog should not be punished after such an incident because it will be unable to understand what it has done wrong. Instead, corrective action should be correlated directly and immediately with the rabbit-chasing.

Harsh disciplinary actions, such as beating, scolding, threatening, refusing to speak, locking up, or refusing food, do not succeed in teaching a dog tasks. They have a depressing effect on the animal and cause an unacceptable disposition.

When such punishments are frequently repeated, the dog loses confidence in the handler. This loss may be seen if the dog shows fear when the handler approaches. A dog that has chased a rabbit should be petted and shown that it is liked when it returns to the handler.

To train dogs to avoid food that was not provided by their handlers, a light electrical current— harmless to the dog—can be tied into pieces of meat or other food in the training area. As the dog attempts to eat the food it receives a light electrical shock—a disagreeable experience. This type of training is continued until the dog indicates it has learned not to accept food anywhere or from anyone but an appropriate person in the normal feeding place. This same method of negative reinforcement can also be used to teach an animal to avoid unsafe areas and circumstances.

Primary and Secondary Training Inducements

Both primary and secondary inducements are used in dog training. The dog's sense of touch is used with the primary inducement, while secondary inducements are oral or gesture commands or other kinds of signals. In using the primary inducement, the dog is shown physically what is expected of it through a variety of methods that include petting, pulls, pressures, jerks, thrusts, or the inflicting of disagreeable results.

A dog can associate the sound of a word with the movement required. For this reason, commands must consistently be given in the same firm, clear, and forceful tone of voice. It makes no difference whether the voice is high- or low-pitched. Also, if possible, one-syllable words should be used for all commands.

Words used to command a dog may be meaningless to a human or could even indicate the opposite of what the dog is expected to do. Some trainers use a foreign language to give commands to dogs that they are training to better help the dog avoid responding to a wrongly given command. When gestures are taught, they are usually given simultaneously with the appropriate voice command. After the dog has become proficient in responding to both commands, gestures may then be used alone. The purpose of the two types of inducements is to teach a dog that if it does not respond correctly to a command, or secondary inducement, it can expect a primary inducement to follow, perhaps in the form of a disagreeable experience. Conversely, a dog that responds properly to a secondary inducement can expect to be petted or otherwise agreeably handled or rewarded.

Repetition is the method by which dogs learn. The same command (secondary inducement) along with the appropriate primary inducement must be given over and over until the desired results are obtained. If an animal makes a mistake by assuming an incorrect position or responds incorrectly to a command, it must be immediately corrected. A dog should never be corrected for clumsiness, slowness in learning, or because of an inability to understand what is expected. Observation, patience, self-control, discretion, and a thorough knowledge of training techniques on the part of the handler are essential in determining what corrections are to be made when a dog makes a mistake. If the handler does not have these qualifications or experience, it may the handler's fault—not the dog's—when the dog makes a mistake or does not respond correctly to a command.

Praise—A Motivating Factor

Another motivating factor essential in dog training is praise. More than any other type of reward, a dog desires the approval of the handler—the leader of the pack. A friendly relationship between the dog and the handler is essential. A dog that does not receive praise or does not like the handler will simply not respond effectively. After every properly executed command, even if it has taken more time than expected, a dog should be rewarded with praise because it will sense that it has performed correctly and will do so again. Also, the dog is more likely to respond properly when next given the same command. Dogs can be praised in many ways. Kind words are effective, as are physical recognition, such as petting or fondling, and a period of playing and romping as a reward. The best method for each animal can be determined by the handler who regularly associates with the dog.

Retraining

After a dog has completed initial training, it should periodically be given refresher training to maintain proficiency. This is particularly important in an industrial or business facility where a dog will normally not have to react to problems as often as in law enforcement. Dogs used in the private sector should be given brief refresher training at least monthly.

1.4.3 TRAINING COSTS

Even though a protection dog must be trained, housed, fed, and cared for, the cost of using a protection dog is not great when compared with the cost of added human staff or certain technology-based security techniques. A user may obtain a dog and then have the animal trained by a company specializing in training protection dogs. Alternatively, the user can purchase a fully trained dog. Also, a trained dog can be rented and then housed and maintained on the premises being protected. It can also be delivered to the work site and picked up daily.

Trainers provide both the dog and the training or else just the training. In the latter case the owner provides the dog. Costs vary depending upon the locale of the training center and the type of training required. It is usually considered best to have the trainer provide the dog.

Patrol

This training includes handler protection, obedience, agility, building and area search, and elementary tracking. Trainers generally prefer to provide the dog as well as the training because they can be more certain that correct dog selection criteria have been met. In the first phase of training (typically four to 12 weeks), the trainer works with the dog alone (without the handler) to prepare the animal for later training with the handler.

The second phase of training unites the dog with the handler and requires about two weeks for the basic patrol course. The cost of such training, excluding travel and living expenses for handlers, ranges from $4,000 to $5,000. The cost of the dog may vary from several hundred dollars to $1,000 or more. For patrol training, most trainers prefer that the dog live in the handler's home.

Detection and Recovery

This type of training can be added to basic patrol or can be provided separately. Detection training can be highly specialized. A single dog is generally not trained to detect both drugs and explosives for two reasons: (1) the possibility of confusing the dog in an actual search, and (2) the need for an aggressive search method when searching for drugs and a passive one for bombs and explosives. A dog that scratches and tears at a container in a search for drugs might be killed (along with people nearby) if it used the same tactics in a bomb or explosives search.

Explosive or drug detection training typically adds another $1,000 to $5,000 to the training cost and adds another four to eight weeks to the training period.

Guard or Compound Work

To train a dog to work without a handler in a confined area costs about $1,000 to $1,500 for a two-week session, not all of which involves the handler.

Some companies provide training at the site of the owner or user. In these cases the trainer is often more disposed to work with a dog already owned by the user.

In addition to the initial purchase and training expenses, other costs that should be anticipated include housing (a kennel), food and vitamins, leashes, grooming equipment, warning signs, and veterinary expenses.

Typically, for a leased dog to be placed in an enclosed and secure environment and work alone as a guard dog when no people are present, the cost is $500 to $1,000 per month.

1.4.4 DEPLOYMENT OF PROTECTION DOGS

A dog represents a great psychological deterrent to potential violators. In addition, a dog is extremely effective in assisting in the location and the holding of violators after a protected area has been penetrated. Dogs, properly deployed, increase protection and can substantially reduce costs by minimizing personnel requirements. Like other protection techniques, dogs should be used in concert with a range of security measures to ensure complete protection.

Use without a Handler

In some cases, kennels rent dogs out daily and deliver them to sites that the dogs then protect without handlers, typically during non-working hours. They may be advertised as being trained, but they may not be trained and may in fact have come recently from animal shelters.

An untrained or cowardly dog may give some protection and act as a psychological deterrent. Most potential intruders will not choose to test how well a dog is trained to attack; they will just avoid any areas protected by dogs. Nevertheless, this section discusses only trained dogs.

When a dog is used without a handler, it is not sufficient simply to turn the dog loose in the area to be protected. The user must also be prepared to accept the responsibility that goes with such a choice. Other concerns include relationships with customers, visitors, the community, and employees, as well as the possibility of unfavorable publicity if the dog attacks a child.

A dog does not think logically, cannot reason, and does not recognize the moral difference between right and wrong. A dog trained to protect a facility without supervision cannot distinguish between an intruder intent on causing harm, such as a burglar, and one innocently entering the property, such as a child chasing a ball. A dog trained to attack is an awesome opponent because it has been taught to keep the premises free of trespassers and to win in any encounter. Serious injury or even death could be the result of an attack.

Because of the danger posed by a dog without a handler, warning signs and structural barriers are essential. Arrangements should be made to have someone who can control the dog respond in case the area is penetrated or the dog escapes. A dog may not give a warning (by growling and barking) but may hide until an intruder has entered the area and then attack savagely. Warning signs posted at frequent intervals around the protected area are essential. They warn potential intruders (to discourage them) and also warn the innocent (to help reduce legal liability).

Structural or electronic barriers are also needed. If an open area is being protected, a well-constructed chain-link fence, at least 8 feet (2.4 m) high, should be installed around it. The fence should be securely fastened at the ground level so a dog cannot dig under it or loosen it. Alternatively, electric fencing can be placed at the bottom to prevent digging. All other areas and openings (such as culverts and drainage ditches at ground level) must also be properly secured.

All openings in buildings must be inspected and strengthened where necessary. A savage, irate, 75–90 lb. (34–41 kg) dog can put great pressure on any surface it attacks. Windows should be secured with bars or heavy-duty expanded metal screens. Doors should be strengthened, where necessary, with metal sheeting or heavy plywood and be securely locked. All fencing and building surfaces should be inspected at least daily to ensure that no areas have become so weakened that a dog might escape.

There are several ways to monitor a protected area to determine when a response is necessary. A simple method is to install a microphone at the site and link it to a central monitoring point. It may also be useful to employ an audio detector with discriminating circuits to screen out irrelevant sounds. A dog bark or growl, or sustained noise from penetration attempts, would cause the detector to transmit an alarm to the central monitoring point. Closed-circuit television might also be installed. Alternatively, security officers on patrol can periodically check the activity of the protection dog as they make their rounds. Of course, only an experienced handler can control the protection dog.

A determined intruder can dispose of a dog protecting an area in several ways. A well-placed shot from a rifle, pistol, or tranquilizer gun can be effective in neutralizing a dog. If a dog has not learned to accept food only at its regular feeding place, it might be disposed of by poisoning. Since a dog has a tendency to become dehydrated easily, it is essential that drinking water be available at all times in the protected area. So, even if a dog has been taught to refuse food, a disabling drug or poison might be put in the drinking water. Finally, if only one dog is protecting an area, one violator might distract it while another violator penetrates the area.

Security personnel should routinely check protection dogs to verify that the animals are still in the areas being protected and that they are in good condition. Also, law enforcement officers responsible for patrolling areas where dogs are used should be aware of their presence and location. They should also be made aware of the danger associated with entering such areas, because protection dogs will attack a law enforcement officer as readily as they will attack anyone else.

Another approach is to lease the dog. Suppliers can provide a kennel on the user's premises and provide food and water daily. During the facility's working hours, the dog is locked in the kennel away from personnel. The kennel can be equipped with a remotely operated door, which can be activated by the last employee to leave at night. The dog then remains free and alone until the scheduled time—usually in the morning—when the supplier visits the premises, cleans up after the dog, renews food and water, and returns the dog to the kennel.

Use with a Handler

Dogs used with handlers are usually more highly trained than those that protect areas on their own. An animal that is taught to work with a handler is taught to respond only to the handler's commands. Such a dog is under the complete supervision of the handler, and a well-trained dog of this type can work around people without endangering them. When properly used with handlers, dogs greatly increase the likelihood of detecting intruders, and their mere presence is a deterrent. A handler and dog must be trained together before going to work. A dog working with a handler (a dog team) is commonly used in these applications:

- foot and vehicular patrol
- apprehension
- tracking
- building and area search
- parking lot surveillance
- personnel and funds escort
- crowd control
- substance detection
- maintenance of custody

Patrol

A dog team may patrol on foot or by vehicle. On foot patrol, a dog team normally is used for routine building, parking lot, and area checks. A dog usually has sufficient stamina to work a regular shift with a security officer. However, a dog can easily become dehydrated in hot weather. The handler must remember this limitation, rest the dog in the shade when necessary, and provide adequate drinking water.

Very cold weather presents different problems, such as the accumulation of ice between the pads of the paws. The hair between the pads should be trimmed short when the team works in snow for prolonged periods. While on patrol in bad weather, the handler should keep the dog on a leash.

When a dog is used on vehicular patrol, special provisions should be made for its health and safety. For example, the seats in an automobile are not well adapted for dog transportation. The upholstery will become dirty and permeated with odor. It also gathers dog hair and may be torn by the dog's claws. In addition, a dog cannot sit or stand comfortably on regular seats because of the lack of traction and hence may tire when riding for long periods. The most practical vehicle for a dog is a station wagon or van because the interiors are hard, resistant to odor, and easy to clean. If a sedan is to be used, the back seat can be removed and a plywood platform or cage assembly installed to accommodate the dog. The platform should be installed about 2 ft. (0.6 m) below the back windows, and can be covered with carpeting to provide traction and comfort for the dog. A small hand vacuum can be used to clean the area.

When on vehicular patrol, a dog may be off-leash but should be required to remain in a "sit" position. The dog should not be allowed to place its head outside the car windows while the vehicle is moving because of the danger of injury from insects or foreign objects. While on patrol, windows on both sides of the vehicle should be open about four inches to provide cross ventilation. If the dog is left in a parked vehicle, the windows should be opened far enough to allow the head out. The handler should never be out of sight of the dog in a parked vehicle. Before the dog enters a vehicle, it should be on a leash and should be required to sit until given the command to enter. Before leaving the vehicle, the dog should be on a leash and taught to remain in the vehicle until commanded to leave.

Apprehension

A well-trained dog is particularly valuable during an apprehension. If a violator has been discovered and attempts to escape, the handler releases the dog from the leash and gives necessary commands for the dog to pursue and attack the violator or to hold the violator. When the individual being apprehended is stopped, surrenders, and is being held by the dog, the handler then gives the command for the dog to release the violator. The apprehended individual is then directed to move slowly back, generally about 10 ft. (3 m). The dog is ordered to sit. Finally, the individual is informed that the dog will attack without command if the suspect attempts to escape or attacks the handler.

A dog that has been taught to work with a handler has usually learned that the only time to attack without command is when a violator who is already apprehended attempts to escape or attacks the handler. If the apprehended individual is to be searched, the dog remains in a sitting position until the search has been completed. If violators are to be taken into custody and escorted on foot, handlers place themselves about 10 ft. (3 m) behind and about 2 ft. (0.6 m) to the right of the apprehended individuals. The dog is off-leash and placed to the left, so that the dog is directly behind the violator. The dog is in a position to attack immediately if the individual being escorted attempts to escape. If the apprehended individual is to be transported in a vehicle, handlers position the dog between themselves and the offender.

If an individual surrenders without attempting to resist or escape, the same procedure is followed. However, in this instance the dog would immediately be placed in a sitting position, off-leash, while the handler proceeds with the necessary steps required to search the person and take him or her into custody.

Tracking

Protection dogs are usually not specifically trained in tracking. To search for a person who has been missing for some time, a dog specifically trained for such work should be obtained.

Of course, even protection dogs have an excellent sense of smell, which can be used to good advantage to track and capture a suspect who is attempting to escape apprehension or who has only recently left a location. The dog should be allowed to smell any available articles, such as clothing, with the suspect's scent. Next the dog should be taken by its handler to an area where it will have the best opportunity to pick up the suspect's scent; it should then be encouraged to track.

Tracking success depends to a great extent on the amount of time that has elapsed, because the strength of the scent diminishes as time passes. The ground surface also affects tracking success. A dog can track better in grass and brush because human scent adheres well to those surfaces. Paved or gravel areas and overpowering scents such as fertilizer, burned grass, or spilled oil and gasoline impede a dog's tracking ability. Human scent remains longer on cool, moist ground. Human scent dissipates rapidly in direct sunlight, on extremely dry ground, and in excessive rain.

Building and Area Search

The dog's senses of smell and hearing can be effective in searching a room, a building, or an area such as a parking lot or storage yard. The dog is most effective when worked off-leash because its movements are not restricted and it can search a larger area in less time. As a liability and safety matter, prior to releasing the dog within an area, the handler must announce in a loud, clear voice that the dog will be released if no one appears within a specified time. This precaution allows a suspect to surrender and protects innocent persons. If no one appears within the specified time, the dog is released to search. The handler should allow the dog sufficient time to check and clear each area before proceeding. The handler then follows the dog, using the same precautionary warning for each uncleared room or area.

In some cases, a dog may fail to find violators because they are well hidden. However, when violators hear the warning that a dog is being released, they often come out of hiding and surrender.

Parking Lot Surveillance

Dog teams can use vehicle and foot patrols to detect and apprehend intruders in parking lots. A team should patrol in a vehicle for a period and then patrol on foot. During darkness, when there is no activity in a parking lot, the team should patrol by moving in an upwind direction. If the dog alerts, the handler should challenge individuals for identification and apprehend them if they are committing an unlawful act. Should a person attempt to escape or evade apprehension, the handler may release the dog to pursue and attack or hold.

Escort of Funds and Personnel

During transportation of funds or other items of value, a dog with a handler can deter robbery and provide additional protection if an attempt is made. If the dog team is escorting a fund custodian, the team should be slightly to the rear of the custodian so that it can readily observe any hostile acts. If a robbery is attempted, the dog is released and commanded to attack. While in a vehicle, the funds custodian should sit in the back seat, with the dog team in the front.

In addition, a dog team can provide excellent protection when escorting personnel, such as employees who must walk to isolated parking lots at night.

Crowd Control

In settings where crowd control is necessary, dogs provide an effective psychological impact. The mere fact that a dog is in the area may encourage crowd members to behave in an orderly manner. Dogs in such situations are normally kept on a leash. If necessary to restore order, dog teams can assist in splitting a crowd, apprehending leaders, or clearing a street or area.

Substance Detection

A single dog can be trained to patrol, protect areas, and detect substances, but usually substance detection becomes a specialty because of the necessary training time. Dogs can be trained to detect such substances as drugs, explosives, or accelerants used in incendiary fires.

Maintenance of Custody

A dog can maintain custody of one or more people who have been apprehended or who are grouped in an area. If those people are in a room or other contained space with a single exit, the animal can be positioned at that exit and ordered to hold them in the space or attack any person who attempts to leave. Such a tactic can only be used briefly and only if the people involved are unarmed.

Even if the people are in an open space, the animal's speed will ensure that the first to attempt escape will be attacked. In this situation the dog would be commanded to hold the group and attack any person who moved. In an emergency or while awaiting help from other security personnel, a dog team could maintain custody in this way, even if the handler had to leave the dog briefly.

1.5 SPECIAL APPLICATIONS AND SKILL SETS

Dogs can be trained to detect drugs, explosives, fire accelerants, and people. When used for tracking, trailing, or substance detection, dogs require the assistance and direction of a handler. The handler plans the search and takes steps to optimize the dog's capabilities. To effectively combine the handler's intellect and the dog's sense of smell, the dog and handler should be trained as a team.

It is generally recommended that a dog be trained for either protection or detection. Dogs required to do detection work undergo constant retraining that is different from and may conflict with protection training. For example, a detection dog is usually fitted with a special leather collar so that when the collar is placed on the dog, it knows it is going to work.

1.5.1 TRACKING AND TRAILING

In tracking, a dog is given a scent article and then follows the same scent through the air or as left on grass, trees, leaves, etc. The dog also smells ground disturbances—that is, crushed or disturbed vegetation or marks on the ground. In trailing, the dog uses only the first technique, following the left-behind scent in the air.

Tracking and trailing dogs are motivated by a natural instinct for prey. However, to insure focus and dedication to the unique tasks assigned, a tracking dog should not be allowed to chase game.

The bloodhound is a renowned tracking dog, but other breeds are equally proficient, such as the German shepherd, Doberman pinscher, Airedale, rottweiler, Irish terrier, Labrador retriever, schnauzer, beagle, golden retriever, and Malinois. Dogs with flat noses, such as the mastiff, boxer, and bulldog, are generally not as well suited for tracking. Also, housedogs that are usually kept indoors and have close contact with people do not make optimal tracking dogs because their sense of smell is diminished by being in the artificial environment of a household.

Training a dog for tracking and trailing takes about two years and can usually be done only by an expert through continuous, consistent, and challenging training.

Sensing Techniques

Every person has a unique scent that a dog can distinguish. Perspiration, the most distinctive scent in humans, contains various glandular acids. As a person passes through an area, these chemicals are left on the ground and in the air. (Interestingly, when a person has been drinking alcohol, the perspiration has a different scent, one that is disagreeable to dogs.) Feet generate much perspiration, which passes through shoes and clothing while a person walks.

Hands also leave a scent, but almost all trails are left by the feet. Though the perspiration odors of hands, feet, and underarms differ, their scents are closely related and can be easily followed by a dog.

Perspiration is not the only scent a dog can sense. For example, the layers of earth uncovered from a footprint are usually damper than the undisturbed surface of the soil, and because of evaporation where the foot falls, the smell of earth is stronger. The strength of such a track scent is variable because the pressure of footprints may differ. If undergrowth is present and plants are trodden down, the strength and character of the plant smells may provide the dog with useful information. Shoe polishes, too, may leave detectable scents.

Terrain and Weather Conditions

Ground type and weather conditions affect a dog's tracking and trailing ability. It is hard to track and trail on dusty, sandy, or stony ground and on dry pavement. Damp sand can hold a scent in favorable weather for as long as 12 hours. On ground that is overgrown with grass and vegetation, a track will hold in moist air, moderate winds, and no sunshine for as long as 24 hours. Dry air conditions, a high wind, and hot sunshine in regions without shade can sometimes obliterate a track in three hours. Tracks made after sunset often remain in good condition until the next morning before the ground dries. If snow falls on existing tracks, the track scents sometimes hold until the fresh snow is about 1.5 in. (3.8 cm) deep. Although a scent will hold in a slightly damp atmosphere, downpours and rains of long duration will extinguish a track scent.

Temperature also affects tracking ability. Dissipation of the scent occurs faster when the temperature is high. The early morning or late afternoon hours are the most favorable tracking periods for a dog. Also, humidity, which improves the scent, is usually lower during peak temperature periods. Conflicting smells, such as fumes produced by smoke, chemicals, or fertilizers, reduce the dog's ability to detect and follow a track. Traffic of all kinds should be kept away from the track so strange scents will not confuse the dog. Although a dog follows a track with its nose to the ground, as it nears the objective it may change from track scent to body scent. It then approaches the objective with lifted muzzle while following the scent cone—the pattern of scent dissipation. (A strong breeze carries the scent in a narrow pattern far downwind, while a weaker breeze carries the scent in a wide pattern but not as far.) From this change in the dog's operation, an experienced handler can determine when the dog is approaching the objective.

Terrain features and man-made structures also affect the scent cone. Scent cannot pass through trees, bushes, large rocks, and high grass but must go over, under, or around them.

Scent-carrying wind hitting the crest of a hill may break up into two or three scent cones. Mountains, buttes, gorges, depressions, buildings, walls, and fences may cause the scent cone to sweep and swirl about. Pockets of dead, scentless air may be encountered at the leeward foot of a hill. A dog following a body scent may lose the scent and have to return to the track scent. The ideal scent cone is one that is blown over a flat, even surface with no obstacles.

A trained dog working from a boat can scent a person who is under the surface of the water and breathing through a hollow reed or length of tubing. The U.S. Navy has trained dogs in this technique to locate underwater intruders. Dog teams also work to locate people buried or trapped after earthquakes, landslides, avalanches, and mudslides.

1.5.2 CONDITION OF THE DOG FOR TRACKING, TRAILING, AND DETECTION WORK

When starting a pursue task, the dog should be fresh and not excited. Excitement is apparent when the dog's mouth is open and its tongue is out. In this condition, the dog cannot keep its nose to the ground to trail. A proven technique is to pour fresh water over the dog's nose before the start of trailing to wash away any dust particles that might be lodged in the channels of the nose.

A tracking or trailing dog must be trained not only in pursuit but also in obedience. The dog must be retrained regularly to maintain effectiveness. Training equipment for tracking includes a collar and a leash about 10 yards (9.1 m) long. The dog is usually kept on the leash during tracking so the handler can follow closely. The handler must be prepared to help the dog and to interpret any signs the dog may give during the task. Also, the handler must be in sufficiently good physical condition to keep up with the dog as it works the task.

In addition, the dog must be eager to perform, intelligent, healthy, have a stable temperament, and be eager to please the handler. Although most of the working dog breeds are acceptable for detection work, the German shepherd is the favored breed in the Americas and most of Europe. The olfactory ability of the German shepherd, along with its intelligence and willingness to work for an intangible reward, are this dog's most desirable traits. The Malinois and some other breeds have also proved effective in this type of work.

1.5.3 DETECTING DRUGS, EXPLOSIVES, AND ACCELERANTS

Dogs are the most efficient method for detecting drugs, explosives, and accelerants in most situations.

Training a Dog for Detection Work

Teaching a dog to detect drugs or explosives is time-consuming and requires a professional trainer. The dog is taught the tracking scent by incorporating the scent into a ball or other object the dog will chase and retrieve. When the dog responds correctly, encouragement and rewards are given. The exercise is repeated until the dog learns to locate and retrieve any article containing the scent. A formula for the training regimen is this: odor + response = reward.

The tests increase in difficulty to develop the dog's ability and interest. In addition, during training and in actual searches, the handler uses a special leather collar, which the dog associates with the search. The collar is adjusted so it slips on and off the dog without being unbuckled. It is placed on the dog at the beginning of each exercise and removed as soon as the task ends. A detection dog must have continuous, daily training to maintain peak proficiency—perhaps two hours per day.

Dogs that will search for explosives must be trained not to paw at or otherwise attempt to retrieve an explosive once it has been located. Because of the danger of detonation, dogs must instead be trained to sit and bark to alert the handler. Likewise, dogs must be trained not to come into direct contact with drugs, which can be harmful or fatal to the dog if swallowed.

Basic training for detection work runs six to eight weeks, plus one or two weeks more to train a detector team. It takes about nine months to a year before a handler and a dog become highly effective together in pursuing the more difficult detection challenges.

Drug Detection

The techniques of drug, explosive, and accelerant detection are different from those used in human tracking and trailing. The spirit of the chase is reduced, and instead of casting about for a scent and then following it to the objective, the dog must search for the scent in a prescribed, detailed manner. The task is demanding and often boring because the dog may work for long periods without detecting a scent.

Noise and activity in an area may distract the dog. If a search continues for a long time, the dog may become tired and lose interest. A detection dog can normally work effectively for 20 minutes to one hour. If the dog loses interest and the handler cannot motivate it to continue, it must be given a break.

The detection reliability of a well-trained dog exceeds 95 percent. Also, dogs can search an area rapidly. For example, in about two minutes a dog can conduct an explosives search of a 50-yard (45.7 m) corridor of lockers. When searching for drugs, a dog can search a vehicle in about 1.5 minutes, 125 packages in about seven minutes, and 50 boxes in about three minutes. Dogs can detect drugs themselves as well as the trace odors drugs may leave behind.

Frequently, criminals attempt to mask a drug's scent with the odor of perfume, gasoline, or formaldehyde. They may also employ artificial distractions, substances that have an odor so similar to that of the drug that the dog might give a false alert. For example, artificial distractions that might confuse a dog trained to detect marijuana include oregano, alfalfa, parsley, and other spices. Any substance that contains acetic acid can confuse a dog searching for heroin.

With adequate training, however, most dogs learn to disregard artificial distractions completely. It is reasonable to expect the average drug dog to detect the presence of a half ounce (14 g) of marijuana or a small amount of opium in a vehicle, a package, an item of luggage, or a room of reasonable size.

Explosives Detection

An explosives detection dog can recognize the scents of common explosives, such as the following:

- **Commercial dynamite.** This is usually found in two forms:
  - *Gelatin:* a sticky or rubbery dynamite of nitrocotton, such as collodion cotton dissolved in nitroglycerin and nitroglycerin gel.
  - *TNT (trinitrotoluene)*: composed of nitrogen, hydrogen, carbon, and oxygen, made by nitrating the chemical compound toluene.
- **Smokeless powder.** This is a mixture of sulfur, charcoal, and nitrate—either sodium or potassium graphite—coated during manufacturing to reduce static electricity.
- **C-4 plastic explosive.** This consists predominantly of Research Department Explosive (RDX) in a plasticizer mixture. C-4 is an odorless, white to light brown, putty-like material.
- **Others**. Dogs may also be trained to detect the following substances:
  - black powder (powder form, time fuse, safety fuse)
  - detonating cord (PETN [polyerythrytoltetranitrate]-based)
  - detonating cord containing RDX (cyclotrimethylene trinitramine)
  - binaries (such as Kinepak)
  - black powder substitutes
  - blasting agents
  - cast boosters
  - Composition-B
  - emulsions and slurries
  - water gels
  - plastic explosives (such as Semtex)
  - tetryl
  - improvised explosives (ANFO [ammonium nitrate and fuel oil], chlorates, nitrates)

Figure 1-2 lists items that have caused dogs to alert falsely.

Item that Can Cause a False Alert	Remarks
Stainless steel insulated bottle	The bottle was owned by a heart patient who took nitroglycerin pills and handled the bottle after handling the pills.
Back of television; jet instrument panel	Some circuit boards are coated with a shellac containing nitrocellulose. Dogs often alert on items painted with this shellac.
Grease pencils	Grease pencils contain nitrobenzene as a softening agent.
Shoe polish	Shoe polishes may contain nitrobenzene or nitrotoluene as a preservation and softening agent. Nitrotuluene is a by-product in the synthesis of TNT and is also used in some plastic explosives.
Blackboard chalk labels	These labels are covered with a shellac containing nitrocellulose to prevent smudging.
Pure glycerin	The glycerin molecule is similar to that of pure nitroglycerin.
Cakes	Maraschino cherries in some cakes are flavored with benzaldehyde.

Figure 1-2
Items Found to Cause False Alerts in Explosives Detection

Open Area Search

The same factors that affect a dog's tracking ability—such as wind, weather conditions, terrain features, and man-made structures—also influence a dog's ability to search for drugs or explosives in an open area. The search should be started from the downwind side. The area is then systematically searched using the quartering method, whereby the team works its way back and forth across an area, moving from one end to the other.

Building Search

Wind currents inside a building, too, can affect a dog's sensing ability. Drafts, cross-ventilation, and heating and air conditioning units all affect scent patterns. If possible, these conditions should be controlled by switching off air conditioners, heaters, or fans. Wind and intermittent drafts may cause the dog to alert on the scent but be unable to pinpoint the source.

Before a building search, all personnel should be removed, distracting influences minimized, and the dog allowed to become familiar with the environment inside the building. A systematic search should be conducted in a clockwise direction. If air currents are noted, the handler must watch the dog carefully for an indication of airborne scents. Every item—such as desks, cabinets, bookcases, ventilation ducts, and other equipment—must be checked. Each area should be cleared—judged as clean—the first time it is checked. Thus, the dog must to search high (walls, lockers, tables) as well as low (under chairs, along baseboards).

The handler should encourage the dog throughout the search, especially when the dog is required to jump or stand to sniff a particular location. The handler may also assist the dog by touching and showing the dog items to be searched. The handler must consistently recognize a dog's alerting signal.

Vehicle Search

A vehicle search should begin from the downwind side and continue clockwise. The dog should pay particular attention to fenders, wheels, wheel wells, hubcaps, and bumpers. If the dog shows interest in the inside of the vehicle, the handler should let the dog go so it can search the seats, floor, and dashboard. The handler must be particularly aware of the dog's alert signal because the dog may have difficulty showing it in the confined area. If an alert is noted, the handler should help the dog sit.

The dog will encounter the most difficulty when searching the engine compartment from beneath. Because of insecure footing, cramped working conditions, and the danger of being burned on a hot engine, special care should be taken when working the dog in these areas. The handler should be especially patient and helpful and provide encouragement to the dog. For example, if a dog is trained to sit to alert when an explosive is detected, it may become confused because of the lack of room to sit underneath the vehicle. In this situation, the handler must then coax the dog out and encourage the dog to sit. However, one must never encourage the dog to respond; such encouragement is known as a cue.

Aircraft Search

The procedures for searching aircraft are essentially the same as those for building searches. Aircraft present many distractions: odors from humans, food, and other sources; noises peculiar to an aircraft and its support equipment; and vehicle movement nearby. The aircraft should be searched away from structures and personnel in an open area where the wind velocity is high. All power equipment associated with the aircraft must be turned off before the search is started.

One method of searching an aircraft is to approach the aircraft from the downwind side and search its exterior. The most accessible parts are the landing gear, wheel wells, and cargo hold.

The handler must check for suspicious objects that would be out of the dog's reach. If possible, the dog should search the cargo hold with the baggage inside. If that is impossible, the baggage must be unloaded and checked separately; then the cargo hold can be searched. Also, ground support units—such as generators, power units, and vehicles—may have to be searched.

Next it is time to search the aircraft interior. Ideally, the doors should be closed and ventilation systems turned off to allow a scent to saturate a specific area instead of filtering throughout the aircraft and possibly confusing the dog. In extremely hot weather, one door should be opened. If several doors are open and air is flowing through the aircraft, the handler must watch the dog for any sign of an airborne alert and encourage the dog to follow it to its origin.

If the search is started from the front of the aircraft, the cockpit should be cleared first. Next the handler should scan the passenger compartment for likely places of concealment. A back-and-forth, side-to-side pattern should be followed at the back and front of each row of seats, and the area underneath must be checked. Also, the dog should climb onto the seats and search the overhead storage areas, as well as any equipment storage compartments used by the crew.

Galleys must also be searched. Food preparation devices may be hot, so the handler must ensure that these devices do not injure the dog. Also, food and spices in storage compartments may interfere with the search.

Restrooms are the most confining spaces for a dog to search. It is best to allow the dog to search these areas off-leash. To ensure a thorough search, the handler must observe the dog and guide it to possible places of concealment.

Accelerant Detection

Accelerant detection canines have been used to locate ignitable liquids since 1987. The dogs are trained to help investigators locate the exact spot from which to collect a fire debris sample that has a high probability of containing ignitable liquids. The value of using an accelerant detection dog is its ability to discriminate between pyrolysis products—fire debris—normally found at a fire and pyrolysis products that contain an ignitable liquid. Labrador retrievers are especially adept at this type of detection.

In accelerant detection training, a dog is exposed to the odor of 50 percent evaporated gasoline. The dog is trained to assume a sit position when an ignitable liquid is detected. (A food reward is used to reinforce this response.) The dog is trained daily to discriminate between normal pyrolysis products and those that contain an ignitable liquid. Through daily training, the dog can achieve over 95 percent accuracy. Of course, the canine alert alone is not proof that a crime has been committed. Such proof requires a concerted effort by the fire investigator, dog handler, and laboratory technician.

Accelerant detection dogs can be used to search fire scenes, equipment, vehicles, and crowds. At a fire scene, the mobility and the keen olfactory sense of the dog can significantly reduce the time required for the fire investigator to complete the investigation. Without an accelerant detection dog team, the fire investigator would take a large number of samples for analysis from a search based on fire behavior and burn patterns. However, the investigator may overlook an area in which the perpetrator poured an ignitable liquid that did not burn. The trained dog can significantly reduce the number of samples required and ensure that unburned liquid areas are not overlooked.

The search of a burned vehicle can result in multiple alerts by an accelerant detection dog. It is up to the investigator to determine whether an ignitable liquid would normally be located in any particular part of the vehicle. The dog can also search the vehicle for physical evidence used by an arson suspect.

An arsonist will frequently remain at the fire scene and mingle with onlookers. The accelerant detection dog, which is normally very friendly and will not pose a danger to people in the crowd, can be taken through the onlookers in an effort to detect the scent of ignitable liquids. If the dog alerts, the investigator can question the individual to determine why the dog alerted. If a suspect is identified, and all legal requirements are met, the suspect can be placed in a lineup with people who do not have ignitable liquids on or near them. The dog then searches the lineup to identify the person with the scent of ignitable liquids.

An arsonist will usually dump a liquid container or other physical evidence into a nearby field or wooded area. Compared to humans, an accelerant detection dog can search the area faster and better.

1.5.4 COSTS

Most enterprises use tracking, trailing, and substance detection dogs only infrequently. Renting such dogs as needed is usually the most cost-effective approach.

A tracking or trailing assignment generally costs $1,500 to $2,000 for a 24-hour period. The cost of a canine search for substances varies with the type of substance to be detected and the number of dogs and handlers required. A search for drugs with a single dog might average $1,000 per day. A search for explosives involving a large area or several airplanes might require several dog teams. If six dog teams are needed, for example, the basic cost may average over $4,000 per day.

1.6 LEGAL LIABILITY

The use of dogs in assets protection operations can result in significant criminal or civil liability for injuries.

1.6.1 CRIMINAL LIABILITY

The following questions can help in determining the risk of criminal liability:

- Does any statute make the ultimate conduct a crime, including criminal negligence, which is different from the civil tort of negligence?
- Is the intentional use of a dog to achieve a purpose or engage in conduct defined as a crime?

Criminal liability occurs when one party, without justification or excuse, causes his or her dog to attack another person. In the jurisdiction in which the attack occurs, if it would be a crime for the first person to attack the second person with his or her own body or with a weapon or other object, then using the dog to make the attack would also be a crime. In general, the animal can be viewed as a weapon or an extension of the handler. It is the conscious human use of the dog that, in court, establishes intent.

1.6.2 CIVIL LIABILITY

Regarding civil liability, the main questions to examine are as follows:

- What conditions or circumstances might give rise to civil liability?
- What relationships among the various parties may alter the existence or degree of liability?
- What special legal doctrines apply to the conditions and relationships so as to produce unusual or extraordinary results?

Conditions and Circumstances

The conditions and circumstances that trigger liability are those under which the animal will come into contact with or affect a person or property. In assets protection, the following conditions and circumstances are typical instances in which liability may arise:

- **When the dog is at leisure or not on duty.** The dog may be resting between tours, confined to its usual quarters or kennel, or at large but not specifically for protection purposes (such as when it is being exercised).
- **When the dog is on duty.** The dog is actually being worked—on or off leash, with or without a handler—in connection with a protection assignment.

- **When the dog threatens a person.** The dog attacks, barks, or otherwise induces fear in a person without an actual physical attack.
- **When the dog physically attacks a person.** The dog physically attacks and actually makes contact with a person.
- **When the dog sets in motion an intervening instrumentality.** For example, the dog knocks over an object by running into it, and the object injures a person or creates a fear of injury.

Relationships

The conditions and circumstances above have a different significance depending on the relationships between those involved. The following are types of relationships that might be encountered with a trained detection dog:

- The person injured is a trespasser on the property protected by the dog.
- The person injured is a licensee[2] on the protected property.
- The person injured is a business visitor.[3]
- The person controlling the animal is the person whose property is being protected, such as a homeowner or proprietor.
- The person controlling the dog is an employee of the property owner or person being protected.
- The person controlling the dog is an independent contractor or the employee of an independent contractor.

Special Legal Doctrines

Several legal doctrines and topics relate to liability in the use of dogs in assets protection. For example, a dog can be considered a dangerous weapon or instrumentality.[4] A dangerous instrumentality is any instrumentality so constructed or used as to be likely to produce death or great bodily harm. A person using or setting in motion a dangerous instrumentality is strictly liable for the consequent damage or injury. Moreover, a person who is strictly liable will be held liable despite efforts to control the instrumentality or prevent the undesirable

---

2 A licensee is one who has express or implied consent to enter land for his own purposes and not for any purpose or interest in the possessor (*Black's Law Dictionary*, 1979).

3 A business visitor is one who is invited or permitted to enter the premises of another for a purpose directly or indirectly connected with business dealings between them (*Black's Law Dictionary*, 1979).

4 *Commonwealth v. Tarrant*; *Green v. Ross*.

effects from occurring. Large protection dogs specifically trained to intimidate, deter, attack, and apprehend will probably be considered dangerous instrumentalities.

A dog can be considered dangerous or vicious if the dog owner or controller knew or should have known of the dog's vicious propensities (Prosser, 1971, Section 76). A person who controls or possesses a vicious animal must exercise due care to prevent that animal from causing harm or injury to innocent people. A protection dog that has attacked or caused injury in the past—irrespective of whether the object of the attack was innocent—is likely to be considered a vicious animal, even if the dog is trained to be aggressive only on command. Currently, most cases hinge not on whether the dog was vicious but on whether its use in the circumstances constituted reasonable force.

One who has control of a property or premises is obliged

- not deliberately to cause or permit harm or injury to any person on the property without legal justification and
- not to allow an invitee or business visitor to be injured or harmed by any event or circumstance of which the person in control was aware or ought to have been aware (*Restatement of Torts*, 1977, Section 332).

1.6.3 LIABILITY REGARDING TRESPASSERS

The use of a protection dog against a trespasser may or may not trigger liability. The following are examples of the application of liability in various circumstances:

- If a trespasser—a person knowingly present without a right to be so or with an unlawful intent—entered the property, the dog could be used to detain, apprehend, or control the trespasser to the same extent that the owner or person in control of the property could. Therefore, reasonable force—short of deadly force—could be used against the trespasser to prevent or halt the trespass.
- If a protection dog bites or otherwise injures a trespasser and the trespasser has not performed a violent act or used force, the actions of the dog likely constitute unnecessary force.
- In the instance of unnecessary force, both the dog handler and property owner would be held liable for damages. The handler would be liable for intentional use of excessive force or for negligence (that is, failing to prevent the use of unnecessary force by the dog). The owner would be liable under the theory of vicarious responsibility for the act of the handler (the owner's employee) or under the theory of strict liability for a dangerous animal or dangerous instrumentality.
- If the trespasser was seriously injured by a protection dog after the dog merely apprehended the trespasser, and the trespasser responded by attacking or provoking the

dog, there would be no liability because the attack on the dog would be considered a provocation. Under the common law doctrine of vicious animals, a provocation that caused the animal to attack would be enough to remove the animal from the class characterized as vicious (similar to the doctrine of self-defense). Under the dangerous instrumentality doctrine, the trespasser would have caused the foreseeable reaction by provoking the animal. Thus, the trespasser would not be entitled to protection or owed a duty of care.

A key element in liability for the owner or controller of a protection dog is the existence of reasonable fear on behalf of the trespasser. If the trespasser truly felt the dog was going to attack, and such a fear could be proven, then a reasonable defense against the anticipated attack would be permitted. In such a case, it could be held that the trespasser did not, according to the law, provoke the animal and that the animal's attack was excessive force for which the owner and controller would be liable.

A canine attack on an invitee[5] or business visitor[6]—if not provoked by the person—would result in legal liability to the handler and property owner. The law imposes a higher duty of care for the visitor than the licensee; however, a developing doctrine treats all people present with express or implied permission as invitees to whom a duty is owed to prevent foreseeable injury. The extent of damage or harm for which the defendants will be liable would be a question of fact. The natural sympathies of jurors can be anticipated to lie with the person innocently attacked by the dog, leading to an increase in monetary damage awards for the plaintiff.

1.6.4 PRECAUTIONS

Those who use dogs in assets protection can take several precautions to reduce the risk of criminal or civil liability:

- **Select the protection dog with care to ensure it is trainable, stable, and appropriate for security work.** The dog should be trained by a competent professional and should be trained to respond in the least damaging way consistent with the circumstances. Thus, a command to hold would be more appropriate than one to attack. (It is not the precise language used but the conditioned and expected animal response that determines whether the dog's actions were legally permissible. Even so, words like "attack" could have an undesirable impact on a jury.)
- **Be certain the dog is under control when working where an innocent person might be harmed.** If patrolling premises when people are legally present, such as during working

5 Zareb v. Frederick; Flynn v. Lindenfeld.

6 Tompson v. Wold; Carrow v. Haney; Dobrin v. Stebbins.

hours, the dog should be under physical restraint (a leash) except in response to a genuine security emergency or one reasonably thought to exist.

- **Place the public on clear notice of the dog's presence.** Such a warning should also forbid entry to all but those specifically authorized. This prominent, double warning also warns trespassers, to whom a lesser degree of care is owed. The warnings should be in the language or languages that the public would most likely understand.
- **Assume that the protection dog will be regarded either as a dangerous instrumentality or a vicious animal in any litigation resulting from the dog's use.**
- **Procure adequate liability insurance, or if self-insured, provide adequate resources for this potential liability.**

The discussion of liability is not intended to discourage the prudent use of assets protection dogs, as a properly trained dog is often the best resource to use. However, for any security measure, all costs should be considered, and the cost of liability insurance is merely added to the acquisition, training, and deployment costs of the dogs. These costs should be proportionate to the risk-reduction achieved. In the current litigious environment in which security operations function, it is most prudent to take every reasonable precaution to minimize liability.

REFERENCES

Black's law dictionary (5th ed.). (1979). St. Paul, MN: West Publishing Co.

Carrow v. Haney, 203 Mo. App. 485.

Commonwealth v. Tarrant, 314 NE (2) 448 (Mass).

Dobrin v. Stebbins, 122 Il. App. (2) 387.

Flynn v. Lindenfeld, 6 Ariz. App. 459.

Green v. Ross, USDC, Florida, 338 F. Supp 365.

Nutrient requirements of dogs: Revised 1985. (1985). Washington, DC: National Research Council.

Prosser. W.L. (1984). *Law of torts* (5th ed.). Eagan, MN: West Publishing Company.

Restatement of torts (2d ed.). (1977). Philadelphia, PA: American Law Institute.

Tompson v. Wold, 47 Wash. 2d 782.

Zareb v. Frederick, 138 F.2d 689.

CHAPTER 2

HIGH-RISE STRUCTURES: LIFE SAFETY AND SECURITY CONSIDERATIONS

2.1 INTRODUCTION

This chapter applies information from the *Protection of Assets* volume on physical security to address life safety and security considerations for high-rise structures. Additional material regarding the concepts and principles that are discussed can be found in other chapters of *Protection of Assets*.

2.1.1 WHAT IS A HIGH-RISE STRUCTURE?

Generally, a high-rise structure is considered to be one that extends higher than the maximum reach of available fire-fighting equipment. In absolute numbers, this has been set variously between 75 feet[7] (23 meters) and 100 feet (30 meters), or approximately 7–10 stories (depending on the slab-to-slab height between floors). As one source notes (Craighead, 2003, p. 1):

> The exact height above which a particular building is deemed a high-rise is specified by the fire and building codes[8] in the area in which the building is located. When the building exceeds the specified height, then fire, an ever-present danger in such facilities, must be fought by fire personnel from inside the building rather than from outside using fire hoses and ladders.

---

7 "NFPA 101 [Life Safety Code] defines a high-rise building as a building more than 75 ft (22.5 m) in height where the building height is measured from the lowest level of fire department vehicle access to the floor of the highest occupiable story. This definition is consistent with many model building codes, but it should be noted that many different definitions exist in local jurisdictions that use varying height and measurement criteria" (Holmes, 2003, p. 13-19).

8 A code is defined as "a systematic collection or revision of laws, rules, or regulations. Strictly, a code is a compilation not just of existing statutes, but also of much of the unwritten law on a subjects" (*Black's Law Dictionary*, 2004, p. 253).

The world's first high-rise structures were built in the United States around the end of the 19th century. Since that time their design and construction has changed, resulting in the skyscrapers that today dominate the skylines of most major cities throughout the world.

Although the world contains different types of tall structures, this chapter considers the high-rise to be essentially an office building, located in an urban or metropolitan area, accessible directly from one or more public streets, and having a mixed occupancy with public assembly areas, retail spaces, and conventional offices.

2.2 LIFE SAFETY CONSIDERATIONS

2.2.1 SPECIAL CONCERNS OF HIGH-RISE STRUCTURES

The risk, or "the possibility of loss resulting from a threat, security incident, or event" (ASIS *General Security Risk Assessment Guideline,* 2004, p. 5), is a function of factors such as the facility size, the number of occupants, and, for intentional threats,[9] the value[10] of the target.

For a high-rise structure the risks and potential losses are higher due to the large size of occupied floor areas, potential difficulties in responding to and containing threats, and the inability to effect immediate evacuation of an entire building. (Because of the limited capacity of building stairwells and elevators, not all occupants can simultaneously leave a facility. Also, in some incidents—especially fires—elevators serving the affected floors are not usually considered a safe means of occupant escape.)

The ability to mitigate threats for high-rise structures depends on structural design and the use of technology to deter and detect a threat, to communicate its nature and location, and to initiate automatic or organizational responses. The concepts for life safety protection are similar to those for the development of a security program: planning must address identified assets at risk, and solutions should follow the principles of deter, detect, delay, and respond.

Life safety protection is primarily mandated by codes, particularly those for building and fire. At first glance this would appear to simplify decision making, but the standards[11] are

---

9 "[A]n intent of damage or injury; an indication of something impending" (*ASIS General Security Risk Assessment Guideline,* 2004, p. 5).

10 In the case of terrorism, the value of the target to terrorists may include its status within a city or country and its type of tenants. For example, if the targeted building is a symbol of economic strength or is the tallest building in a city, a "successful" terrorist act will achieve the perpetrator's goals, i.e., widespread publicity.

11 A standard is "a model, type, or gauge used to establish or verify what is commonly regarded as acceptable or correct" (*Webster's New Universal Unabridged Dictionary,* 2nd ed., as quoted in *Protection of Assets,* 1999).

designed for minimum protection only and their interpretation often requires a code expert and clarification from the local authority that enforces the law or regulation.

Life safety issues can have impacts on security. The security manager for a building may be tasked with both functions even though, at times, the functions may have opposite goals. For example, life safety mandates that all occupants be permitted unimpeded egress from an area; however, security would rather not permit a thief, who has stolen property, to have such freedom to escape. Creative access control measures, conforming to applicable life safety codes, are often required. (See further discussion later in this chapter.)

Life Safety Aspect

The most critical threats[12] in high-rise structures include fire, explosion, and contamination of life-support systems such as air and potable water supplies. These threats can be actualized accidentally or intentionally, and because they propagate rapidly, they can quickly develop to catastrophic levels.

The most significant factors affecting life safety in high-rise structures are as follows:

1. Early detection and precise location of incipient hazards
2. Reliable communications throughout the structure and with outside agencies
3. Assurance of safe escape routes
4. Prompt application of appropriate control measures (such as fire extinguishment, containment or replacement of contaminated air, shutoff or filtration of drinking water, and containment and removal of explosives)

Fire is given special attention in high-rise structures. Buildings tend to contain large amounts of combustible material, and the potential that a serious fire could move upward (particularly if the structure is not protected with an automatic sprinkler system) is ever-present. As one source observes:

> Despite the fact that fires are rare occurrences, if one does occur, everyone in a building must react quickly. In other emergencies, such as a winter storm or civil disturbance, the initial reaction to early warnings of this type of emergency will not necessarily determine its impact on the building. In a fire emergency, however, the first 3 to 4 minutes are critical. The timely handling of a fire emergency according to sound procedures can help stop the event from rapidly becoming a major problem (Craighead, 2003, p. 308).

12 Ensuring the safety of individuals can involve threats that may include crimes, such as robberies or assaults, or may be related to building emergencies such as elevator entrapments, power outages, or natural disasters.

Building Vulnerability Aspect

Structural integrity and essential utilities and services such as lighting, communications, elevators and escalators can be threatened in the event of a fire or an explosion. Various threats to high-rise structures can spread upward, downward, or horizontally. Fire, for example, can spread to higher floors because of the natural tendency of heated gases to rise. But if combustible materials (such as wall and floor coverings) follow a downward path, fire may spread in that direction. Fire may also spread horizontally within a floor, particularly in the absence of adequate floor-to-ceiling walls and partitions. In major conflagrations, without early containment and suppression, fire may spread in all three directions. With explosions or sustained conflagrations, partial or total building collapse may cause multiple injuries and deaths.

Contaminants in the air supply, such as smoke[13] or chemical or biological agents, can travel with the air from the point of entry through its distribution pattern. If that pattern involves return and recirculation, contaminants can be repeatedly distributed over the same areas unless they are filtered or the distribution system is shut down. If a single air-handling unit serves multiple floors, contamination can affect all the floors served by that unit. Depending on the air handling system, contaminants may travel upward, downward, or horizontally on any involved floor.

Contaminants in the water supply move with the water from the point of introduction. Successful attack on a water supply system can be difficult because any opening in a charged pipe will cause a leak. But if a valve or control point is found and water flow is stopped temporarily, the contaminant may be introduced downstream of the valve and will move in the stream when the valve is reopened. If such a point could be found near the beginning of the distribution piping, it would be possible to contaminate a major portion of the system. Gases and solids dissolved in a solution can be delivered in water to outlets such as sinks, drinking fountains, and toilets. Heavier contaminants might collect in traps and adhere to pipes but also might be released at outlet fixtures. For highly toxic agents, the degree of exposure could be enough to cause serious harm. Even if only a small quantity of a highly lethal agent is introduced, its effect could be widespread because of sustained use of the water before the contamination is detected.

Communications facilities within a high-rise are usually routed through common vertical risers for the entire height of a structure and distributed horizontally from junction or service ports on each floor. In wire systems of this type, a complete severance of the applicable cable could halt all service downstream of the cut-point and could also affect use upstream by interrupting the direct path. Disruption of communications both inside and outside a building may have dire consequences, particularly affecting emergency communications.

---

13 "[T]he total airborne effluent from heating or burning a material" (Clarke, 2002, pp. 8-9).

For that reason, alarm signal and communications systems should be distributed so that localized points can operate independently even when communication with a central control panel or processor has been disrupted.

Threat of Bombing

Life safety planning must also consider bombs. The risk that an occupant, visitor, or a delivery person could introduce a quantity of explosive material into a building is possible. The use of screening equipment, such as explosive detectors, X-ray machines, and metal detectors, can mitigate such a threat. Rigorous vehicle control procedures can reduce the possibility of a large quantity of explosive material being transported into an under-building or subterranean parking area or loading dock. However, in a crowded urban environment, it is difficult to prevent the destruction that could be caused by a bomb-laden vehicle parked close to a building.

For new construction, one possibility is to design structures to withstand the detonation of a defined quantity of explosive without progressive failure of the structure. Maximizing the distance between a parked vehicle and the building—i.e., setback—is important, as is window design. Unfortunately, such solutions involve cost that needs to be justified by the probability[14] of such an occurrence. For existing buildings, the cost of these solutions may be prohibitive, although some improvement in the distance between parked vehicles and the building can be achieved through the use of heavy planters, bollards, and other such barriers and parking restrictions. Also, security film can be applied to existing windows to reduce the possibility of flying shards of glass, which can cause serious injury and damage.

In assessing whether a particular facility is at risk to a bombing, the following questions should be considered:

1. Is the building a likely target (such as being a landmark that may attract attention)?
2. Are any tenants in the building a particular target for domestic or international terrorists?
3. Is the building an obvious easy or soft target due to poor security measures?
4. Are any nearby buildings a likely target? (And, therefore, could collateral damage be caused by an explosion at a close-by building?)

14 "[T]he chance, or in some cases, the mathematical certainty that a given event will occur" (*ASIS General Security Risk Assessment Guideline*, 2004, p. 4).

In many cases, the likelihood that a particular building will be a target is minimal. However, emergency management plans, including the evacuation preparedness of tenants, should be up-to-date and rehearsed so that if such a threat does materialize, the building is prepared to properly respond. Such preparation is particularly important for high-rise structures, compared to low-rise. A single-story building provides speedy emergency egress for occupants via multiple horizontal paths, whereas egress from an upper floor of a high-rise necessitates the same horizontal paths of travel, plus vertical descent via elevators (if available and safe to use[15]) and building stairwells. Stairwells may become congested if total building evacuation is occurring. Also, descending many flights of stairs may be physically taxing for occupants with full mobility and virtually impossible for the disabled or physically challenged without the assistance of others or the use of mechanical evacuation devices, such as chairs.

2.2.2 DEALING WITH THE LIFE SAFETY PROBLEM

The threat of fire and fire-related events obviously affects both people and property. Many countermeasures that aid life safety can have a direct impact on the protection of assets. Anything that assists safe response to an emergency contributes to total asset protection, in particular, the life safety of a building's occupants. However, some emergencies that appear as threats to life safety may be diversions designed to permit unimpeded access to, or attack on, physical assets. A good illustration involves an office building in which the building emergency exit stairwells are normally locked from the inside of the stairwell (in order to prevent reentry to a floor) but are equipped with a fire detection system that automatically unlocks the doors when a fire alarm occurs. A knowledgeable intruder could cause an event, perhaps by activating a manual fire alarm station,[16] which would trigger the automatic response and thereby provide access to a selected location via the stairwell. During such an incident, occupants would more likely be concerned with responding to the perceived emergency and not with securing physical assets, making the attack more likely to succeed.

Such an illustration does not suggest that the fire life safety system should not be required to automatically unlock stairwell doors in such an emergency. The primary concern is life safety, and unless an emergency is clearly known to be a hoax, life safety measures must take priority. The illustration does suggest that complete reliance on locked stairwell doors as an access control measure in a building equipped with automatic unlocking mechanisms is not wise.

---

15 In many emergencies, particularly those involving the threat of fire, elevators are not usually considered a safe means of evacuation and therefore emergency exit stairwells are often the only means of escape.

16 Manual fire alarm stations are also known as manual fire alarm boxes, manual pull stations, or manual pull alarms.

Additional protection must be added to increase the reliability of the locked fire stairs[17] as a control measure. This problem is further discussed later in this chapter.

Local Code Compliance

The first step in assuring life safety is to comply with local building and fire codes applicable to the structure. However, a building, particularly an older structure, although conforming to local codes at the time of construction, later may not necessarily reflect either the most advanced or the best approach to life safety.[18] The building may require subsequent changes to bring it up to date and into current compliance.

In regard to cost considerations, meeting or exceeding current code requirements may achieve concessions elsewhere that offset the increased cost. For example, reductions in commercial insurance premiums or the stated amounts in funded reserves for the expense of retained risks may be possible.

Fire Detection

This must rank as the first priority. Fire detection—more properly, the detection of products of combustion or the combustion process—is the first step in any response that ranges from confinement to extinguishment to evacuation and escape.

Fire detection must take into consideration the special nature of a high-rise structure; that is, it must be accurate in indicating where a fire is and what stage it has reached. Fire codes have long required that manual fire alarm devices be located on each floor of a multi-floor structure in the normal path of exit from an area. However, reliance on such a system alone is not sufficient. If, for example, someone who detects a fire on the fourth level of a facility immediately runs down the stairs and on the way out of the building activates a main lobby fire alarm pull station, what does that say about the fire? The fire alarm system could say "Fire in Lobby"—the logical inference from the location of the pull station. That might prompt the wrong response. A manual pull station ensures that people have an opportunity to signal a fire emergency and warn other occupants while escaping, but it does not ensure that the emergency area will be accurately identified. The answer does not lie in eliminating or relocating manual devices, but in augmenting the system with detection mechanisms that help determine the exact location of the fire emergency. The following means of fire

17 Fire stairs are "building emergency exit stairwells" (or more commonly "building stairwells") or a "stair tower." "The name reflects the traditional reason for evacuation, which has been building fire" (*Emergency Evacuation Elevator Systems Guideline*, 2004, p. 45).

18 In addition, municipalities, which adopt specific editions of standards into law, may not update the law in a timely fashion when the relevant standard changes.

detection should be distributed throughout a high-rise structure to optimize early and localized detection. (Also, see the *Protection of Assets* volume on physical security for additional information on fire detection sensors.)

Smoke Detectors

Smoke detectors are automatic fire detection devices designed to detect the presence of smoke. One source describes them as follows (Craighead, 2003, p. 187):

> Smoke detectors generally are located in open areas, spaces above suspended ceilings, spaces under raised floors (particularly in computer rooms and data centers), cafeteria areas, air duct systems, passenger and service/freight elevator lobbies, elevator shafts, elevator machine rooms, enclosed stairways, dumbwaiter[19] shafts, chutes, and electrical and mechanical equipment rooms. The specific locations and spacing of smoke detectors are determined by an assessment of local laws, codes, and standards and engineering issues.

Even an incipient fire, controlled before structural burning, could have costly consequences in many interior spaces within a high-rise facility.

Heat Detectors

Heat detectors are automatic fire detection devices designed to sense a certain temperature or rapid change in temperature. The *Fire Protection Handbook*[20] notes (Roberts, 2003, p. 9-17):

> Heat detectors are very reliable and have the lowest false alarm rate of all automatic fire detectors. They are best suited for fire detection in small confined spaces where rapidly building high-heat-output fires are expected, in areas where ambient conditions would not allow the use of other fire detection devices, or where very early warning of fire is not required.

Sprinkler and Standpipe Alarms

Where standpipe and hose systems and automatic sprinkler systems have been installed, water-flow and valve-position alarms are appropriate. A standpipe system in a high-rise building is designed to transport water vertically to upper floors of the building so that a fire can be fought manually with hoses. A sprinkler system is defined as (Puchovsky, 2003, p. 10-189):

---

19 "[A] hoisting and lowering mechanism, used exclusively for carrying materials, with a limited size car that moves in guides in a substantially vertical direction" (Donoghue, 2003, p. 12-204).

20 Quotes in this chapter from the *Fire Protection Handbook* are used with permission from the National Fire Protection Association.

> a combination of underground and overhead piping that is connected to an automatic water supply and is installed throughout the building. The piping is specially sized or hydraulically designed with that portion of the piping within the building generally located overhead. Sprinklers are attached to the overhead piping in a systematic pattern and a valve controlling each riser is located either directly on the system riser or in the supply piping. The system is usually activated by heat from fire and discharges water over the fire area. A device actuating an alarm when the system operates is located on the system riser.

Nature of Fire Alarm Systems

Modern fire alarm systems are computer-based and are similar in systems architecture to security alarm systems. Field devices, such as smoke detectors and air-handling controls, connect to field panels, which connect to the main computer. Some of the field devices may be connected in a long series but still be individually addressable, using, for example, individual names that they report when communicating their status.

Some codes prohibit the fire alarm system from performing any function other than fire life safety and further prohibit the use of any component or device that has not been approved for fire life safety applications. Depending on local authorities, this may preclude the use of fire alarm systems to monitor or control security devices and may also preclude the use of a security system to monitor or control a fire life safety device.

Where such restrictions are in effect, the mandatory release of certain electrified locking devices (normally controlled by an access control/alarm monitoring system) during a fire emergency requires careful design coordination of the systems. Typically, the fire alarm system may not send a signal directly to the security system or its field panels but controls an approved relay that connects to an approved lock power supply. All the associated wiring must meet code, and the lock itself must be fail-safe (i.e., designed to unlock under any failure condition, such as when power is removed).

Fire Extinguishment

Automatic sprinkler systems are an essential aspect of fire protection for high-rise structures. As the *Fire Protection Handbook* notes:[21]

> When sprinklers are present, the chances of dying in a fire and property loss per fire are cut by one- to two-thirds, compared to fires reported to fire departments where sprinklers are not present. ... When sprinklers do not produce satisfactory results, the reasons usually involve one or more of the following: (1) partial, antiquated, poorly maintained, or inappropriate systems; (2)

21 "U.S. experience with sprinklers" by K. D. Bohr, National Fire Protection Association Fire Analysis and Research Division, as reported in Hall, 2003, p. 2-21.

explosions or flash fires that overpower the system before it can react;[22] or (3) fires very close to people who can be killed before a system can react.

Other Fixed Systems

Standpipe and hose systems are typically found in tall and large-area buildings (Shapiro, 2003, p. 10-351). They consist of small hose connections and perhaps hose racks for internal use, along with larger connections for fire department use. The *Fire Protection Handbook* notes:

> Standpipe systems can significantly improve the efficiency of manual fire fighting operations by eliminating the need for long and cumbersome hose lays from fire apparatus to a fire. Even in buildings that are protected by automatic sprinklers, standpipe systems play an important role in building fire safety by serving as a backup for, and complement to, sprinklers. (Shapiro, 2003, p. 10-351)

In addition to water (the primary agent for extinguishing fires in most high-rise structures), extinguishing agents include dry chemical and wet chemical systems, carbon dioxide, halon and halon replacement systems,[23] which have specialized applications in such structures. Dry chemical and wet chemical systems are used mainly for restaurant hoods, ducts, and cooking appliances found in kitchens and cafeterias. Halon, halon replacements and, in certain situations, carbon dioxide, are used in electrical switchgear rooms and in computer and data processing installations. In a building equipped with water sprinklers, the cost of other separate fixed systems and the estimated cost of likely damage in the event of activation of that type of system should be compared with the cost of sprinkler protection and the likely cost of sprinkler system water-related damage.

Smoke Control

Smoke can be hazardous to people and property, including a building itself and its contents. One obvious way to control smoke is to limit the use of flammable synthetic materials in modern furnishings and furniture. Such materials should, if possible, be kept to a minimum, and only those of a fire-resistive quality should be permitted in buildings. Of course, the proliferation of personal computer systems in the workplace has made the limitation of combustible materials all the more difficult. Smoke control measures are affected by the design and construction of a building. The *Fire Protection Handbook* notes:

---

[22] In the September 11, 2001, New York World Trade Center attack, the Twin Tower's automatic sprinkler systems, particularly those at or near where each place hit, were destroyed by the impact or rendered ineffective by the burning fuel.

[23] Halon production ended January 1, 2000, "except to the extent necessary to satisfy essential uses, for which no adequate alternatives are available" (Taylor, 2003, p. 6-281). Existing stocks can be recycled until they are exhausted. A number of halon replacements have been developed as alternative agents to halon.

> Smoke can behave very differently in tall buildings than in low buildings. In low buildings, the influences of the fire, such as heat, convective movement, and fire pressures, are generally the major factors that cause smoke movement. Smoke removal and venting practices reflect this behavior. In tall buildings, these same factors are complicated by the stack effect, which is the vertical natural air movement through the building caused by the differences in temperature and densities between the inside and outside air. This stack effect can become an important factor in smoke movement and in building design features used to combat that movement. The predominant factors that cause smoke movement in tall buildings are stack effect, the influence of external wind forces, and the forced air movement within the building.[24] (Milke, 2003, p. 12-116)

Forced air movement is caused by a building's air-handling equipment and air-conditioning and ventilating systems. Heating, ventilating, and air-conditioning (HVAC) and air-conditioning and ventilating (ACV) systems are found in most high-rise buildings.

As one writer observes, "Air-conditioning and ventilating systems, except for self-contained units, invariably involve the use of ducts for air distribution. The ducts, in turn, present the possibility of spreading fire, fire gases, and smoke throughout the building or area served"(Webb, 2003, p. 12-237). Therefore, "the location of equipment and the fresh air intakes, the types of air filters and cleaners, the system of ducts and plenums,[25] and the use of fire and smoke dampers[26] are crucial in limiting and containing a fire"(Webb, 2003, p. 12-242).

It is not possible to thoroughly address such a complex subject as smoke control within the scope of this chapter, particularly as the operation of systems designed to control smoke movement vary substantially from manufacturer to manufacturer and building to building and also differ according to the laws, codes, and standards in effect at the time the system was installed. However, generally speaking, there are two basic approaches to the issue. To restrict the spread of fire and smoke throughout a building or area "the HVAC system can be shut down and the fire area isolated or compartmented.[27] Another approach is to allow fans

---

24 The movement of smoke in high-rise buildings can also be complicated by post-construction building modifications that result in improperly sealed openings in floors. Called poke-throughs, when they are small and installed to permit telecommunications or other wiring or ducting to pass between floors, such openings permit smoke to mitigate. If such openings occur on enough floors, the building's air handling system can be impaired.

25 A plenum is "a compartment or chamber to which one or more air ducts are connected and that forms part of the air distribution system. It can be used to supply air to the occupied area or it can be used to return or exhaust air from the occupied area" (Webb, 2003, p. 12-241).

26 Fire and smoke dampers are installed in air conditioning or ventilating ducts to automatically restrict the spread of fire and smoke, respectively.

27 "Barriers such as walls, partitions, floors, and doors with sufficient fire resistance to remain effective throughout a fire exposure have a long history of providing protection against fire spread. These same barriers provide some level of smoke protection to spaces remote from the fire" (Milke, 2003, p. 12-120). Compartmentation also includes the automatic closing of fire doors, such as elevator or lobby doors.

to continue to run, using the air duct system for emergency smoke control"(Webb, 2003, p. 12-241). Moreover, "in many high-rise buildings, when a fire alarm occurs, there is automatic pressurization of stairwells using [mechanical] fans that keep smoke out of the stairwells"(Craighead, 2003, p. 207).

Fire Department or Emergency Services Notification

When an incident involving a building's fire life safety system occurs, the fire department or emergency services must be notified immediately. In addition to notification by assigned staff at the building, monitoring of the fire life safety system by an off-site central station or by the fire department itself may be required by local code or may be an additional life safety measure taken by the building owner or manager.

Occupant Notification

When a fire or fire alarm occurs in a high-rise structure, it is critical that all affected occupants and responders be notified promptly. As the *Fire Protection Handbook* notes:

> Fire alarm systems ... protect life by automatically indicating the need for the occupants to evacuate or relocate to a safe area. They may also notify emergency forces or other responsible persons who may then assist the occupants or assist in controlling and extinguishing the fire. Audible and visual notification appliances alert the occupants, and, in some cases, emergency forces, and convey information to them (Schifiliti, 2003, p. 9-35). A fire alarm system that simply sounds an audible signal [in the form of bells, sirens, and whoopers] and flashes strobe lights in a space is conveying a single bit of information: fire alarm. Systems that send voice announcements[28] or that use text or graphic annunciators typically convey multiple bits of information. They may signal a fire alarm and give a specific location and information on how and where to evacuate or relocate ... When provided with detailed information about a fire emergency, people tend to evacuate more quickly and effectively ... Audible and visible appliances may also be used to indicate a trouble[29] condition in the fire alarm system, or they may be used as supervisory signals to indicate the condition or status of other fire protection systems, for example, automatic sprinklers" (Schifiliti, 2003, p. 9-35).

A public address (PA) system is a one-way system that allows voice communication from the building's fire annunciator and control panel (located in many high-rise structures in a room known as the fire command center or fire control room) to occupants of the building.

---

28 Announcements may be live or prerecorded, depending on the requirements of the local authority.

29 A trouble signal "indicates a fault in a monitored circuit or component of the fire alarm systems or the disarrangement of the primary or secondary power supply" (Moore, 2008, p. 14-5).

Emergency Planning

To adequately address the life safety of a high-rise structure, it is essential that a comprehensive emergency management plan be created. An emergency management plan describes the actions to be taken by an organization to protect employees, the public, and other assets against threats from natural and man-made hazards. In developing an emergency management plan, managers anticipate possible threats and design initial reactions ahead of time so that, in an emergency, they can focus their time and efforts on the most important actions required.

For a high-rise structure, the plan should address such issues as the following:

- posted evacuation signage that clearly marks the means of escape from areas within the building
- description of the types of building emergency systems and equipment and how they operate
- the nature of the building emergency staff organization (including building management and the building fire safety director; engineering, security, janitorial, and parking staff; and floor response personnel such as floor wardens, or fire wardens, and other necessary persons, including those responsible for assisting disabled persons) that will handle emergency response until outside response agencies arrive
- contact details for persons and agencies needed in an emergency
- procedures for building emergency staff to handle each emergency expected for the building, including the methods of evacuation and relocation[30]
- how building occupants, floor wardens and building emergency staff are trained in life safety, including the frequency and nature of evacuation drills—commonly known as fire drills

Of course, the plan must be kept up to date in order for it to be effective.

[30] The need to evacuate or relocate occupants depends on the nature of the emergency. For most high-rise emergencies, it is not necessary to evacuate occupants to the outside of a building but rather to conduct a staged evacuation whereby they are relocated to an area of safety within the building nor is it necessary, except under extreme circumstances, to conduct a total evacuation of all building occupants.

2.3 SECURITY CONSIDERATIONS

2.3.1 SPECIAL CONCERNS OF HIGH-RISE STRUCTURES

Previously, this chapter addressed the special concerns of high-rise structures from a life safety perspective. Concerns from a security perspective will now be looked at. As one source observes (Craighead, 2009, pp. 28-29):

> From a security perspective, high-rise buildings differ from low-rise buildings in these ways:
>
> 1. The existence of multiple, occupied floors, one on top of another, usually[31] means a higher concentration of occupants and therefore more property that could be damaged or stolen as compared with that in low-rise buildings. The potential for theft can increase because the concentration of property makes the site more attractive to a criminal; also, the greater the concentrations of people, the better the chances of a thief's anonymity, particularly if he or she dresses and behaves like other building users. Kitteringham noted that, "many tall buildings and high-rises are located in central business districts. Their proximity to mass transit facilities and ease of access to the general public puts them at particular risk from professional thieves."[32]
> 2. The more individuals assembled in one location at any one time, the higher the possibility that one of these persons will commit a crime against another. One of the difficulties in making [such] statements is the lack of crime pattern analyses[33] for high-rise buildings. The incidence of crime in any building, whether it is a high-rise or low-rise, is impacted by factors such as the neighborhood in which it is located, the design of the building, its use and type of tenants, and the security program that is in place.
> 3. In addition, although this may seem self-evident, all high-rise buildings have stairwells and elevators, and a low-rise, single-story building does not. A stairwell, because it is a relatively unused area (apart from use in emergency evacuations), could be the site of a crime, such as an assault (including that of a sexual nature) or a robbery. An elevator also could be the scene of vandalism and crimes against persons.

Access to and egress from high-rise buildings is often funneled through the core of the structure where vertical transportation, such as elevators and escalators, is provided. Authentication and control of ingress and egress requires special consideration. The application of meaningful and

---

31 The term "usually" is used here since some high-rise buildings, depending on their use, may not have a high number of occupants (for example, some residential and apartment buildings and those primarily used to house telecommunications equipment).

32 Kitteringham, Glen K., *Security and Life Safety for the Commercial High-Rise*, Alexandria, VA: ASIS International; 2006, as referenced in Challinger D., *From the Ground Up: Security for Tall Buildings*, CRISP Report, Alexandria, VA: ASIS Foundation Research Council, 2008.

33 Glen W. Kitteringham noted that "crime pattern analysis is a process that encompasses a number of techniques, all of which can assist crime risk management. It is therefore best regarded as a generic term, covering a number of approaches and techniques for analyzing the incidence and distribution of crime" (A pattern for crime: an overview of the two dimensional mapping process for crime risk evaluation. *Canadian Security, Facility Management Supplement*, Aurora, Ontario, Canada; November 2001).

effective security measures for the high-rise building environment helps to minimize the impact of most security threats.

The Problem of Exposed Assets

Significant assets may be at risk in high-rise structures. As the ASIS International Commission on Guidelines has observed (*General Security Risk Assessment Guideline*, 2003, p. 6):

> Assets include people, all types of property, core business, networks, and information. People include employees, tenants, guests, vendors, visitors, and others directly or indirectly connected or involved with an enterprise. Property includes tangible assets such as cash and other valuables [e.g., furniture, fixtures, and art objects] and intangible assets such as intellectual property and causes of action. Core business includes the primary business or endeavor of an enterprise, including its reputation and goodwill. Networks include all systems, infrastructures, and equipment associated with data, telecommunications, and computer processing assets. Information includes various types of proprietary data.

Many of these assets are vulnerable not only to natural hazards but also to theft and malicious damage. In buildings open to the public, the often large number of people moving in halls, corridors, elevators, stairs, and public areas makes the assets' vulnerability even greater.

For the purposes of high-rise protection, it is not relevant that the risk of loss be shared by various organizations. The need for protection flows from the nature of the assets, not from the identities of the owners. If a tenant with a high exposure chooses not to protect its assets, there may be a threat to another tenant because the unprotected assets could attract attackers to the building. The final protection scheme should involve a cooperative effort between the building owner and manager and the tenants themselves.

2.3.2 LIFE SAFETY AND SECURITY DILEMMA

As mentioned earlier in this chapter, the factors that complicate life safety in a high-rise structure can also create security problems. For example, code provisions that require unimpeded exit capabilities at all times when a building is occupied mean that egress may be possible with little or no surveillance. During a genuine emergency, security forces may be unprepared for the joint demands of emergency response and heightened security.

Furthermore, some life safety requirements make it possible for two persons to stage an event that could render a target location within the building vulnerable. One person could simulate a fire emergency on one level by activating a manual fire alarm, and an accomplice, many levels away at the target location, could take advantage of doors unlocked due to the emergency. To maintain security under such conditions, countermeasures can be used. These may include intrusion alarms and video surveillance featuring alarm-triggered camera display and video recording.

The following sections address available security resources and their appropriate applications in protecting high-rise structures. A typical high-rise building is described below for purposes of illustration.

2.3.3 TYPICAL HIGH-RISE

The main ground level lobby of a typical high-rise office building is illustrated in Figure 2-1.

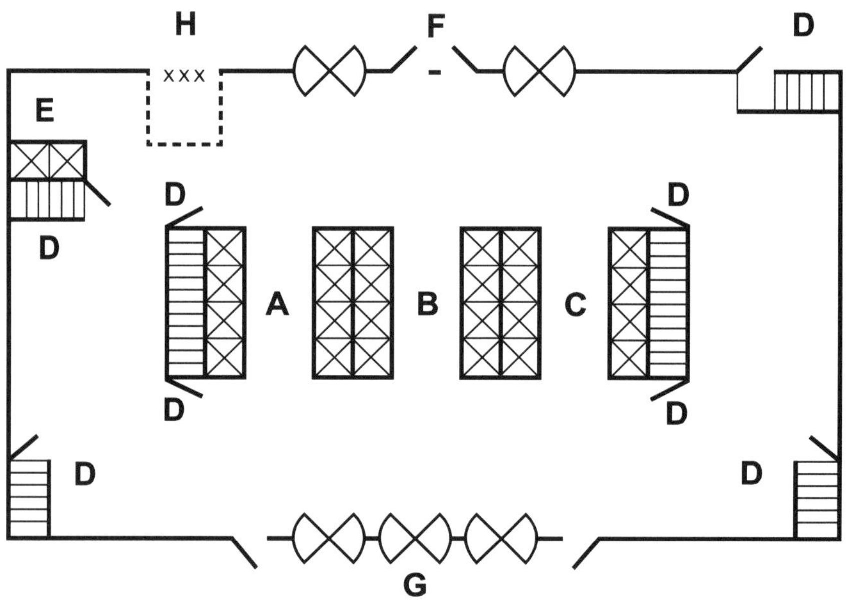

Legend:

A = High-rise elevator lobby (eight cars serve)
B = Mid-rise elevator lobby (eight cars serve)
C = Low-rise elevator lobby (eight cars serve)
D = Fire stair enclosures and doors
E = Service elevators (two cars serve all floors B2 through 40)
F = Rear doors with one set double swinging and two revolving
G = Main doors with three revolving and two single swinging doors
H = Overhead door and ramp down for trucks

FIGURE 2-1
High-Rise Office Building General Lobby

Profile data for the fictitious building are as follows:

- The building is 40 stories high.
- It has about 6,000 occupants divided into roughly 150 occupants per floor.
- The passenger elevators in each of the three banks serve approximately one-third of the building, while the service or freight elevator cars serve all floors, from the basement levels through 40.

The two basement levels, B-1 and B-2, have mechanical and storage areas served by two service elevator cars and the low-rise bank (C bank) elevators. Level B-1 features a vehicle entrance via the ramp shown at H in the figure. The ramp entrance is secured at the street level by an overhead, metal roll-down gate and at the bottom of the ramp by an overhead, open-grille roll-down gate. Inside the area protected by the latter is a loading dock that can accommodate four trucks and is served by the service elevators.

2.3.4 BUILDING OPERATING MODES

Before discussing security measures, it is helpful to understand some common security concepts for high-rise structures. The first is the concept of "open" or "closed" buildings:

1. *"Open" buildings.* Access is typically unrestricted at the building entry level. Tenants, building employees, and visitors proceed directly to their destination floor, via building elevators, where the occupier of that space determines the level of entry control and security. Open buildings may provide a concierge or security desk at the street level to provide directions and deter access by "undesirables"(if they are easily identifiable as such) and to implement security procedures for messengers, delivery persons, and contractors.
2. *"Closed" buildings.* Access to elevator banks at the building entry levels is controlled by some form of credential checking, visitors are authenticated prior to proceeding to elevators, and sometimes a separate messenger center is provided.
3. *"Hybrid" buildings.* Where a major tenant may occupy a large part of the building, one or more elevator banks may be designated as closed, while other elevator banks that provide access for multiple tenants are operated in an open mode.

The second concept is that buildings operate in different modes depending on traffic, occupancy level, hour of the day, and day of the week:

1. *Business hours.* The regular mode of building security operates during regular business hours for the majority of the tenants.

2. *Intermediate hours.* These are usually an hour or two before and after regular business hours and possibly Saturdays, when occupancy is light and enhanced security is required. The building main entry doors may remain unlocked, but tenants and visitors may be more closely scrutinized.

3. *Off-hours or after-hours.* During nighttime, weekends, and holiday hours, when fewer tenants are present, enhanced security is required, particularly when maintenance and cleaning crews are working and special activities (such as tenant deliveries and tenant space modifications) are in progress. The building main entry doors are usually locked, and entry requires a credential, such as an access control card, or the summoning of a building employee or security officer by a signaling device (such as an intercom or buzzer).

2.3.5 BUILDING ELEMENTS

There are systematic ways of viewing a high-rise structure.

The classical approach is to view a property in terms of rings. The property boundary is the first ring, the building is the second, and the specific interior spaces are the third (Healy, 1983, Chapter 3). This scheme needs only a slight variation to fit the high-rise structure: the building line is usually the first ring since, in an urban environment, the building line is often adjacent to a public sidewalk; access to vertical transportation (stairs, escalators, and elevators) is the second ring; and individual floors or floor sections are the third.

For access control purposes it is helpful to divide the high-rise structure into three classes or types of interior spaces:

1. *Public access or common areas.* These include street-level entrance lobbies, main elevator lobbies, access routes to retail spaces and restaurants in the structure, promenades, mezzanines, and, increasingly in new buildings, atria.

2. *Rented or assigned occupancies (i.e., tenant spaces).* These areas are leased or owner-occupied spaces on various floors. Depending on the occupant, such spaces may be open to public access during business hours or may be restricted to identified and authorized persons.

3. *Maintenance spaces.* These include mechanical rooms and floors, communications and utilities access points, elevator machine rooms, janitorial closets, and spaces with strict limited access.

Access control measures are different for each class or type of space, depending on the security program.

Access Control of Public Areas

In order to control access of persons entering the main lobby of the building, such persons need to be categorized. For example, regular tenants may be issued a credential—such as an access control card—that permits rapid verification of their right to enter. However, if visitors need to be authenticated, communication with the visitor's host may be required. Figure 2-2 illustrates some of the categories of persons entering the building and the areas to which they may require access. For areas noted with "?,"access depends on specific building operations and the security level required.

Traffic Category	Retail Space	Loading Dock	Passenger Elevator	Service Elevator	Tenant Space	Fire Exits	Mech., Elec. Mach. Rms	Roof
Retail Tenant	•			?		•		
Retail Customer	•					•		
Office Tenant	•		•		•	•		
Office Visitor	•		•		•	•		
Contractor	•	•	•	•	•	•	•	•
Building Maint.	•	•	•	•	•	•	•	•
Delivery Driver	•	•	?	?	?	•		
Messenger	•	•	?	?	?	•		
Janitorial Crew	•	•	?	•	•	•		

FIGURE 2-2
Traffic Type and Access

A possible control scheme for a building is that access to all floors above the main lobby is controlled by locking the building stairwells or fire stairs against entry from the lobby while allowing free egress to the lobby and placing control points at each bank of passenger elevators. To be completely effective, such a scheme would require that all persons using the elevators to present some form of personal identification and/or permit inspection of inbound property. During periods of heightened security this may be acceptable. However, under normal circumstances, some building tenants may resist such tight security. This is especially true of tenants with walk-in customers. If the building contains a bank, it will generally be located on the ground level and perhaps use part of a basement as well (for its vault and safe deposit areas). Bank lobby access will usually be unrestricted.

If retail operations are restricted to the ground floor and separate street access can be provided, building security need not be compromised. (Such an arrangement is particularly important for a closed building that houses, for example, a restaurant or cafeteria that is open to the public. It is important that visitors be able to enter the cafeteria or restaurant freely but not to have access to the rest of the building.) If, however, a building owner occupies some floors and rents others, it is important to plan the space allocation or stacking arrangement of tenants to facilitate access control at a minimum cost and inconvenience. If, for example, the owner plans to occupy half the building and rent the other half, or make any other allocation between proprietary and rental floors, the building can be operated as a hybrid, and the following security planning points should be considered:

1. *Identify particularly sensitive owner occupancies.* These include executive offices, data processing facilities, cash or securities handling, activities involving large amounts of sensitive proprietary data, and any other space that the owner has designated as critical.

2. *Isolate sensitive owner spaces.* To the degree possible, sensitive spaces should be grouped together on floors that constitute a single sector (low-rise, mid-rise, or high-rise) of the structure.

3. *Impose access controls on the building sector containing the sensitive occupancies.* In the typical high-rise, assume that the owner has chosen to occupy the floors served by the high-rise (bank "A") plus half of the mid-rise (bank "B") elevators, and to rent the others. The sensitive occupancies could be stacked in the floors served by the high-rise bank. If, in the occupancy of the mid-rise sector, the division of floors is about equal, the mid-rise lobby could be divided in half and the mid-rise elevators programmed so that half the cars serve floors 13 through 19, the other half floors 20 through 27. The half serving sensitive occupancies (say, floors 20 through 27) would then be controlled in the same way and probably using the same security personnel controlling the high-rise bank, using card readers and line or other traffic-flow devices. Should the occupancy ratio change in the mid-rise, the controls could easily be abandoned without affecting the high-rise element.

4. *Ensure that controls cannot be bypassed.* If the elevators have been designed so that certain floors are common or "crossover" for two or more elevator banks, it is important to ensure that transfer at such a floor will not permit uncontrolled access to a sensitive area. For example, if floor 27 is served by both the high-rise and the mid-rise cars to permit crossover on that floor, it would be necessary either to install an access checkpoint using security staff on floor 27 or to control access to sensitive floors using card readers in the elevator cars that serve both banks. If no crossover floor is provided, persons who wish to go from the high-rise to the mid-rise or vice versa must descend to the main lobby to transfer to the other elevator bank.

Elevator Control

Throughout the life of a high-rise structure, changes in occupancy may require changes in access control requirements. It is a major advantage if the passenger elevators are originally designed (or retrofitted when that would be cost-effective) to permit access control of all floors. With such control, it is possible to program each car individually as to how it will respond to calls from within the car and from elevator lobbies. Also, the installation of card readers in all elevator cars, even if the readers are not activated at all times, is a sound security measure. An additional security measure to screen persons before they enter an elevator is the use of turnstiles. If, in the future, due to a change in security needs, the building must move from being an open building to be a closed building, the transition can be achieved by programming the elevators to be on card access control 24 hours per day, seven days per week, and issuing access cards to only those persons authorized to access designated floors for time periods determined by tenant management.

Service or Freight Elevators

Service or freight elevators pose special problems in all high-rise structures because they often serve all levels of a building. If they are self-service, the entire building security program may be compromised unless the service cars are

- programmed not to access sensitive floors without special arrangements,
- locked at hoistway doors on sensitive floors, or
- the service elevators arrive on floors where the vestibule or lobby doors are locked, where applicable.

Moreover, service cars offer an opportunity for unauthorized movement of property from or between accessible floors. Assigning an operator to the service cars or making them available only on request to the security operation helps eliminate this possibility. It may also be useful to install card readers in the elevator cars and video cameras in the cars or elevator lobbies. In any event, use of service cars for general passenger movement should be avoided.

Building Stairwells

Building emergency exit stairwells (building stairwells) or fire stairs are part of the public access or common areas and must be accessible for occupants to escape[34] (particularly when building elevators are not available or are unsafe to use, such as during a fire emergency). Two factors control how building stairwells are secured. One is determined by local fire and

[34] Many codes mandate that at least two emergency exit stairwells be provided per floor. This permits evacuating occupants to use a second stairwell if their nearest one is unusable due to emergency conditions.

building code requirements. During times of occupancy, building stairwells must never be locked in the path of egress. The code may, however, allow restrictions on reentry from the stairwell. For example, some jurisdictions permit doors leading from the stairwell to the floor to be locked as long as on every fourth floor the doors are unlocked to allow an occupant to be able to leave the stairwell enclosure. Other jurisdictions permit locking of the stairwell doors as long as they automatically unlock (or fail safe) when the fire life safety system is activated. The other factor is whether inter-floor movement of building occupants via the building stairwells is permitted. Such movement may be argued for (particularly with multi-floor tenants) since it can save time and reduce demands on elevators and energy consumption, and it is more convenient for building occupants to travel between floors. However, such an arrangement may detract from the security of the stairwells themselves. (A better solution, costly as it may be, is to provide an internal staircase serving the needs of the multi-floor tenant.) If use of the stairwells is permitted by the local jurisdiction, the stairwell doors need to be equipped with approved access control devices, such as card readers, as well as intercoms to permit two-way communication by occupants with building security staff. The selection of locking devices for high-rise building stairwell doors is critical if code requirements are to be met. Any such arrangements must be closely coordinated with local authorities. The following quote emphasizes the challenge of stairwell exit doors (Craighead, 2003, pp. 130-131):

> The fact that security and fire life safety are different disciplines, and that their priorities are sometimes in conflict with each other, is nowhere better demonstrated than at the stairwell exit door. ... [T]he need to maintain immediate, [unhindered] exit from the stairwell at the ground level provides an opportunity for a person who has perpetrated a crime within the building to make a rapid exit.

To address the aforementioned issue, some authorities allow installation of a delayed egress locking device that permits, during non-emergency times, a 15- to 30-second delay in opening the emergency exit fire door from the inside of the stairwell at the ground floor exit. Such a locking arrangement can be helpful when used in conjunction with the following:

- an alarm that notifies security staff that a person is trying to exit the location
- an intercom to communicate with the person
- a video camera to view and record the event

The time delay may be sufficient for security staff to intercept the person. These locks must unlock automatically if there is a loss of power to the lock or the building fire life safety system is activated.

Intrusion alarms (explored later in this chapter) are important on stairwell doors. The alarms indicate entry into the stairway and thereby permit a response. Where stairwell doors are generally locked against floor reentry, an appropriate response would be to dispatch a security officer to the ground level door of the involved stairwell and to send a second officer to enter the stairwell at a point above the entry point indicated by the intrusion alarm. That response might permit interception of the intruder while the person is still in the stairwell enclosure. For stairwell doors that are generally unlocked, intrusion alarms on sensitive floors indicate use of the fire stairwell door on those floors. To function properly, building stairwell intrusion alarms (in fact, intrusion alarms anywhere) must be zoned to indicate precisely which door or area has been violated.

Access Control of Interior Floors and Spaces

The preceding discussion dealt with public access areas; however, many floors and interior spaces within floors also require access control. This may be the only control measure, or it may be practiced in addition to general control at the building lobby level.

Programmable elevators permit some degree of floor control. A variant of that approach, even when total floor control is not possible using the elevator system, is to install card readers in the elevator cars to control access to certain floors. Visitors and others without access cards will then require special handling by building security staff. On a floor with few visitors, an escort could provide the required security. On a floor with heavy visitor traffic, a better solution might be to allow free access via elevators serving that floor, and then to provide a floor reception point to screen admittance. In addition, controlling elevator use with access cards requires authorized users to help deter piggybacking or tailgating, whereby an unauthorized person gains entry by accompanying an authorized card holder to a secured location. Such activity can also be controlled using turnstiles near elevators to screen persons before they proceed to an elevator car.

Depending on design, floor reception can often be achieved at the elevator lobby itself. In the building shown in Figure 2-1, one end of the elevator lobby on an upper floor would need to be locked against entry to the floor (perhaps with provision for remote latch release or card entry), and the reception control could be established at the opposite end of the elevator lobby.

In a major integrated security system, staff at the central console could readily exercise remote access control for one or more floors or areas within floors. Access to smaller spaces within individual floors can be controlled with conventional keys, card readers, remote latch release, and communications/surveillance capability, or by a receptionist.

Special consideration must be given to the use of locking devices on doors leading to elevator lobbies on floors above ground level. For example, in many buildings, during a fire emergency—in particular, the activation of an elevator lobby smoke detector, an elevator hoistway smoke detector, or an elevator machine room smoke detector—the elevator cars serving the affected elevator bank automatically return to a designated level or to an alternate floor (if the activation of the elevator lobby smoke detector occurred on the designated level[35]). Therefore, the selection of any locking device for elevator lobby doors is critical because any persons who may be in the lobby when the elevators recall must be able to exit the elevator lobby and proceed to a building emergency exit stairwell. One should check with the local authority having jurisdiction regarding the types of locking devices that are permitted on these doors.

Access Control of Building Maintenance Spaces

Access to critical areas such as mechanical rooms and floors, air-conditioning rooms, fire pump and fire control rooms, telecommunications and utilities facilities (including electrical transformer vaults), elevator pits, and elevator machine rooms can be controlled using selective admittance devices and monitored using intrusion alarms. Each controlled door, if opened other than with the use of an authorized key, automated access device, or remote latch release, would send to a distinctive intrusion alarm a monitoring location designed to initiate a response to the intrusion.

Even in large buildings with multiple maintenance spaces, it is feasible to maintain access control. The limited population of persons requiring such access should be readily identified. In a fully automated system, such persons will use access cards and readers or be remotely admitted using remote latch control, video surveillance, and two-way communication. Even in a smaller structure for which a major integrated security system investment is not warranted, a minimum, low-cost control would involve the following:

- conventional lock on area door
- controlled key issuance
- intrusion alarm, distinctively zoned
- telephone or radio contact by an authorized key holder immediately before or after entry (the need for communication could be eliminated by equipping the intrusion alarm with a shunt switch operated with an authorized key)

The disadvantage of using keys is that they can be lost and compromised.

---

35 "Designated level is defined as the main floor or other floor that best serves the needs of emergency personnel for firefighting or rescue purposes" (Donoghue, 2003, p. 12-203). "The automatic or manual return, or recall, of elevators to a designated level or alternate level" (Dohoghue, 2003, p. 12-202) is known as Phase I operation. Once the elevators have been recalled, they are then available for firefighters' service using a special key. "The provision that allows firefighting personnel to operate the elevator from within the car, or emergency in-car operation, is commonly referred to as Phase II" (Donoghue, 2003, p. 12-2002). Since the use of elevators is for fire department personnel only, not building engineering or security staff, the use of such a key should be strictly controlled and restricted to the purpose for which it was designed.

Utility personnel require access to some of these building maintenance spaces, particularly telephone installers to telephone frame rooms and terminal panels. The problem can still be handled without totally surrendering security control. An installer, regularly assigned to the structure, can be issued a key or automated entry device. For a temporary worker, after identity has been verified, a one-day-only device can be issued; however, its return must be ensured before the worker leaves the premises.

Access Control of Fresh Air Intakes and Telecommunication Services

Access to fresh air intakes and telecommunication services should be protected.

Fresh air intakes. Fresh air intakes for HVAC systems are often located at or near ground level, where they are usually covered with louvered intake screens. These should be protected against introduction of airborne chemical or biological agents. Figure 2-3 suggests an approach using a grille or baffle at 90 degrees to the actual air intake with an intrusion alarm on the grille. Admittedly, the intake suction could still draw vapors from a source placed on the grille. An even better solution is to locate such air intake ports sufficiently far above the ground to make access impossible.[36]

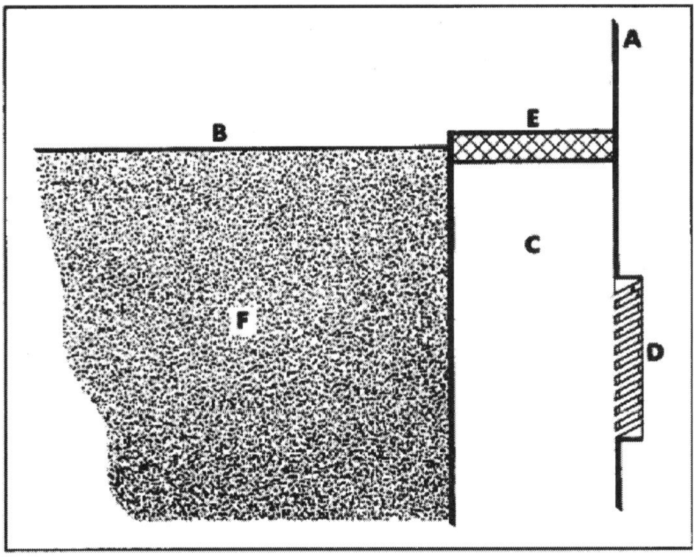

Legend:

A Building exterior wall
B Grade level
C Open space and intake area
D Louvered intake shutter
E Grille (to be protected with intrusion alarm)
F Unexcavated earth

FIGURE 2-3
Fresh Air Intake Protection Scheme

[36] Ways to protect vulnerable outdoor air intakes are documented in Guidance for Protecting Building Environments from Airborne Chemical, Biological, or Radiological Attacks, Publication No. 2002-139 by NIOSH (National Institute for Occupational Safety and Health), Department of Health and Human Services, Centers for Disease Control and Prevention, May 2002, www.cdc.gov/niosh.

Telecommunication services. Telecommunication services typically leave a building in one or more trunk cables and connect with the distribution network in the street conduit and tunnels. Telephone, computer, and alarm systems all use the telecommunications path and are vulnerable to attack along the telephone cable system. For a high-security building, two physically separated paths for telecommunications cable to separate telephone centers are recommended.

The most dangerous or critical points for attack are located at points after all the building services are connected with one or two main trunk cables still in the structure. It is not uncommon in older structures to find such trunk cables exposed in basement or utility area spaces inside the building. In newer structures, usually greater care has been taken to conceal the cables.

It is important to make a careful check of the main cable routes from the communications risers in the building back out through the service entrance. Any access points along the route should be protected. If the cable is in an enclosed space, then intrusion detection devices are required for access points such as hatch covers and doors. If cables are exposed, consideration should be given to hardening the cable path using resistive construction.

2.3.6 SECURITY MEASURES

A number of security measures can be applied to high-rise structures. These include lighting, selective site hardening, building locks and locking devices, alarm sensors, duress alarms, video and integrated security systems, security personnel, and the policies and procedures used to safeguard the assets of a building. More information on these subjects, beyond what follows, is found in the physical security volume of *Protection of Assets* and in the ASIS *Facilities Physical Security Measures Guideline.*

Lighting

Lighting is an important feature in providing protection for high-rise structures. It is a deterrent to criminal activity, including thefts and physical assaults. It can be used for perimeter approaches (such as roadways and pedestrian walkways), perimeter barriers, site landscaping, building facades, open parking areas and parking structures, and all areas within a building, including loading docks. Lighting also aids in the effective use of video systems.

The *Protection of Assets* volume on physical security provides a basic understanding of lighting, the features and benefits of different types of lamps, and the effective application of lighting to increase safety and security.

Selective Site Hardening

An individual or company that is already a high-risk target for criminal attack, including acts of terrorism, may be further exposed in a high-rise structure. In addition to the access control efforts already addressed, there may be a need for specific hardening of a structure at or within particular target floors. Ideally, such security measures should be considered during initial construction, since available options will be fewer in a retrofit and potentially more costly to implement.

Construction features. Resistivity to impact and firearms is a principal reason for special construction. (However, terrorist bombings have added the need to evaluate blast-resistant design for new, high-profile construction.) Materials capable of providing resistivity include standard masonry, blast-resistive reinforced concrete, sheet steel, polycarbonates, acrylic material, compressed fiberglass, ballistic fabrics, bullet-resistive glass, and security window film (to hold broken glass firm, preventing its shards from becoming lethal projectiles). The *Protection of Assets* volume on physical security discusses glazing materials, their resistance to projectiles and bombs, and their reflective properties.

A combination of these materials can be aesthetically integrated into the design to provide protection for the designated space. For example, on a floor occupied by key personnel in the building illustrated in Figure 2-1, both ends of the elevator corridor could be blocked off with resistive material and provided with controlled doors of the same or equivalent material. The partition could be made of masonry and fiberglass, or of steel between conventional drywall panels, and the door could be constructed of resistive glass or polycarbonate. It is less expensive and less confining to total floor architecture if control barriers and hardened materials are used as close to the normal points of floor entry as possible. Hardening and controlling the elevator lobby and all stairwell doors is less expensive than hardening individual offices or spaces within the floor.

Because many high-rise buildings feature dropped ceilings (or below-the-floor spaces) with air-conditioning plenums or ducts that can provide space for intrusion, it is important when hardening selected floors to pay attention to these ceiling (or below-the-floor) spaces. Protection can be achieved by continuing the resistive partitioning to the floor slab above or below, or using heavy gauge wire mesh to close the space but still permit air movement. Intrusion devices are recommended in conjunction with such protection.

Key reception area. If entry control for a target floor is on the floor itself, the reception point must be resistive to attack. However, executives often resist protective barriers around executive floor reception points, saying such barriers convey the wrong message or give a poor impression. Several solutions are available. One is to establish reception on a floor other than the protected floor—perhaps a floor above or a floor below. At that reception point visitors can be identified and their presence communicated to a control person on the sensitive floor. The visitors can then be allowed to proceed to the sensitive floor, which is usually locked against entry, and the control person can then admit them.

Another approach is to create two control points on the protected floor. The outer or reception point would be staffed and separated from the interior floor space by protective barriers in or through which an observation capability would permit a person inside or behind the protected barriers to unlatch the barriers to admit an authorized visitor to the inner area. The guests or visitors would not be aware that the executive floor inner doors were locked against them. The unlatching could be in advance of their movement from the reception area to the door. Although the receptionist would still be potentially exposed, absence of an unlatching mechanism at that point would prevent unauthorized access; one would either have to be admitted by the person inside the protected area or carry a key or other admittance device to open the door from the reception side. The receptionist should not possess such a key or device.

Physical barriers. Various physical barriers can be used to protect structures against threats such as vehicle bombs. These include perimeter fences, walls, sidewalks, pathways, landscaping, fountains, pools, sculpture, benches, planters, barricades, and bollards. The *Protection of Assets* volume on physical security examines structural barriers and the time it may take to breach them. The difficulty is to achieve sufficient spatial separation between the barrier and the structure itself. Since many high-rise structures are located in major cities and towns, where space is at a premium and the structures already exist, this goal is often unachievable. However, properly designed perimeter barriers can keep a vehicle containing explosives from being driven into the structure itself, prior to its detonation.

Parking controllers and barriers can be used to control the entry of vehicles into parking garages and loading docks, particularly those located under buildings.[37] Gate arms and, in higher-security applications, crash-rated hydraulic impact barriers, can be manually or automatically activated to restrict entry to only authorized vehicles.

Building Locks and Locking Devices[38]

High-rise structures use many types of locks and locking devices. The type of locking device used at any particular location depends on the type of door or barrier on which it is

---

[37] Unfortunately, due to insufficient parking spaces in major metropolitan areas, high-rise structures, particularly newly constructed ones, often need to provide under-building parking facilities.

[38] The *Protection of Assets* volume on physical security provides a general description of the different types of locking mechanisms and their relative strengths and weaknesses, as well as information about the specific locks (and locksets) to use for particular applications.

installed and the prevailing building or life safety code requirements. The following are several types of applications and appropriate locks:

- *Building main entrance/exit doors and perimeter legal exit doors: electromagnetic locks.* Using a timer, these locks can be designed to automatically lock and unlock to accommodate the operating requirements of a building. As one source notes, "When the doors are secured, access from the outside of the building can be obtained by hooking up a card reader (normal egress is permitted using panic hardware[39] or automatic unlocking devices such as motion detectors). ... Life safety codes mandate that the power source to all locks restricting occupants' means of egress must be supervised by the building's fire life safety system. In the event of an emergency, such as a power failure or activation of a fire alarm, electrical current to the electromagnet ceases and the doors unlock (i.e., fail-safe). Occupants can freely exit the building and responding emergency agencies, such as the fire department, can enter"(Craighead, 2003, pp. 127-128).
- *Inside of stairwell doors: a special hybrid electric locking device known as a hightower-function mortise[40] lock or stair tower lock.* Such locks were developed so a stairwell door can be locked on the stair side to provide security. A source notes, "Generally, high-tower-function mortise locks are energized and locked at all times. Access control is accomplished by either a mechanical key, digital keypad, or a card reader. ... The power source for these locks is controlled by the building life safety system so that in an emergency, doors immediately unlock yet remain closed and latched, protecting the stairwell from smoke and fire"(Geringer, 1991, p. 2). Also, as was mentioned earlier, some authorities allow installation of a delayed egress locking device that permits, during non-emergency times, a 15- to 30-second egress delay in opening the emergency exit fire door from inside the stairwell. Such locks are required to unlock automatically if there is a loss of power to the lock or the building fire life safety system is activated.
- *Exterior of stairwell doors where they exit the building: key-operated pin tumbler locks and electromagnetic locks.* Stairwell exit doors that normally exit at the ground level "may be locked on the exterior side as long as long as, at all times, the inside of the door is operable, providing uninhibited egress. When an occupant applies pressure to the fire exit hardware,[41] the door will immediately unlock [the exception being delayed egress locks]"(Craighead, 2003, p. 131).

---

39 "Panic hardware devices [such as cross bars and push pads] are designed to facilitate the release of the latching device on the door when a pressure not to exceed 15 lb. (6.8kg) is applied in the direction of exit travel" (Lathrop, 2003, p. 4-72).

40 A mortise lock is one where the lock is set into a mortise or recess in the door itself.

41 "Panic hardware that has been tested and listed for use on fire-protection-rated doors is termed 'fire exit hardware'" (Lathrop, 2003, p. 4-72).

- *Elevator lobby or vestibule doors: electromagnetic hold-open devices.* On activation of the building life safety system, electrical power to each hold-open device ceases, causing it to release the lobby door, which is then free to swing shut and protect the lobby against the intrusion of smoke and fire.
- *Doors leading to tenant spaces: key-operated pin tumbler locks and card access control devices.*
- *Doors inside tenant spaces that do not lead to a legal fire exit: key-operated pin tumbler locks, card-operated locks, token-operated locks, biometric identification system-operated locks, electrified locking mechanisms, and combination locks.*
- *Doors leading to building maintenance areas: key-operated pin tumbler locks, card-operated locks, token-operated locks, biometric identification system-operated locks, electrified locking mechanisms, and combination locks.*

Pin tumbler locks are found throughout high-rise structures. As one source notes:

> The pin tumbler mechanism is the most common type of key-operated mechanism used in architectural or builders' (door) hardware in the United States. The security afforded by this tumbler mechanism ranges from fair in certain inexpensive cylinders with wide tolerances and a minimum of tumblers to excellent in several makes of high-security cylinders. (Edgar, 2004, p. 168)

Pin tumbler locks can be master keyed. The principle of master keying is that a single lock may be operated by more than one key by designing various keys to engage or work on different tumblers or different aspects of the same tumblers. Master keying provides a hierarchy of access to groups of locks, from access to one lock only to access to all locks in the population. The *Protection of Assets* volume on physical security addresses general locking concepts and the recommended methods of maintaining acceptable levels of lock protection. With those principles in mind, the following suggestions are made for the overall lock program of a high-rise structure:

1. *Use interchangeable or removable core locks.* These permit frequent and rapid changes without floor or shop labor. Adequate planning assures that sufficient replacement cores in the various control and master groupings are on hand for immediate use. If a locksmith is on staff, much of the core preparation can be done in-house.
2. *Severely limit the use of a single control or a grand master key.* The obvious danger is total compromise of the locking system through physical loss or loss of accountability of a control or grand master key (or code) or a single core containing the control and grand master combinations.
3. *Use multiple controls and multiple masters.* The building can readily be divided into functionally different units. For example, the low-rise, mid-rise, and high-rise floors

can be regarded as separate locking zones. Each zone can then be set up to its own control and its own master scheme.

4. *Establish multiple key blanks.* In setting up different control and master schemes for major building elements, the key blank style (the profile of the key and keyway) should be different for each of them so that a blank for use in one element will not enter the keyway in the other elements. Such an arrangement helps prevent unauthorized key use. It also makes the same lock combination codes used in one sector available for use in another with low risk of compromise because the key blanks would not be interchangeable.

5. *Set up single zones.* Any distinction by floor or occupancy, or both, will serve the purpose. For example, if the mid-rise is a tenant section, then each of the floors could be provided a separate floor sub-master and all the floors could be included in a zone master. At the same time, spaces within the tenant zone not intended for tenant use, such as maintenance spaces, could remain on separate master systems that are building-wide but confined to a special function, such as electrical, mechanical, or janitorial.

6. *Maintain strict floor master key control.* Sub-master keys at the floor level should be strictly accounted for and issued only to senior personnel of single tenants. If several tenants occupy a single floor, none should have a floor master. Keys issued on this basis should be changed after changes in occupancy.

7. *Keep control of zone master keys.* These keys should be issued on a daily basis only, and only to persons with demonstrated, imperative need. Using multiple zone masters will reduce vulnerability to compromise but not eliminate it. Issuing zone master keys on a day-basis only (i.e., to be returned to security custody before the holder leaves the building) further limits exposure. Choosing very carefully those to be issued with zone master keys (or even allowed temporary custody of them) also narrows the exposure. The carrying of zone master keys as symbols of prestige should be actively discouraged.

8. *Limit access to control keys*[42] *and combinations.* Obviously, no one needs either unless a lock core is to be replaced or a new core pinned. A locksmith will have continuing access to both of these items, so the reliability of that person is of critical importance. Control keys should not be carried at any time except specifically when needed to make core changes.

---

42 Removable core cylinders use "a special key called the control key to remove the entire pin tumbler mechanism (called the core) from the shell [the shell is the cylinder housing]. This makes it possible to quickly replace one core with another having a different combination and requiring a different key to operate. Because of this feature, removable core cylinders are becoming increasingly popular for institutional use, and use in large commercial enterprise where locks are changed often" (Edgar, 2004, pp. 169-170).

9. *Pay particular attention to exterior doors.* These should not be included in any other building master or control system. As they are mostly on ground or below-ground levels, the doors[43] involved will typically lead to specialized maintenance spaces or to public access spaces controlled by the building owner or manager. Exterior doors which are locked against access to the building also require intrusion alarm protection.

10. *Maintain lock quality and complexity of combination schemes.* Although maximum security locks are probably not generally required for high-rise structures with a balanced system of security controls, the locks chosen should be of very good quality. Interchangeable core locks which use a single tumbler (pin chamber) to set up control combinations should be avoided because of the ease of creating a control key given any operating key and a little ingenuity.

Crucial to any locking system is an effective key control system (Finneran, 2004, p. 193):

> Before an effective key control system can be established, every key to every lock that is being used in the protection of the facility and property must be accounted for. Chances are good that it will not even be possible to account for the most critical keys or to be certain that they have not been copied or compromised. If this is the case, there is but one alternative—to rekey the entire facility.

Depending on the size of the structure, rekeying can be a very costly undertaking.

Alarm Sensors

Intrusion detection systems can be deployed in a high-rise structure for various perimeter, stairwell, maintenance, and tenant areas. For example, the following intrusion detection devices can be found in high-rise structures:

- *Passive infrared (PIR) sensors* are used to protect perimeters, areas, and objects; heating, ventilating, and air-conditioning air intakes; interior tenant areas; and building main exit doors (to facilitate automatic opening when occupants leave).
- *Magnetic contacts* are used on perimeter exit doors, building stairwell doors, doors leading to maintenance spaces, and doors inside tenant areas.
- *Break-wire sensors* are used on building heating, ventilating, and air-conditioning air intakes or in interstitial ceiling or floor spaces.
- *Video motion detectors* are used in building stairwells and various locations where video is used in the building.

[43] For security purposes, emergency exit stairwell doors usually should not have locking mechanisms on the exterior of the doors.

Sensor technologies for the detection and annunciation of intrusion are examined in greater detail in the *Protection of Assets* volume on physical security.

Duress Alarms

A duress alarm (sometimes referred to as a panic alarm) is "a device that enables a person placed under duress to call for help without arousing suspicion" (ASIS *Threat Advisory System Response Guideline,* 2004, p. 8). Within a high-rise structure such alarms may be needed in parking garage booths and other cash handling areas, and reception points including executive reception areas. It is crucial that anyone who activates such devices, and those who are responsible for responding to such alarms, be trained to do so according to sound policies and procedures. Also, it is imperative that the operation of such devices be tested regularly.

Video Surveillance

Video surveillance is a cost-effective security feature to help protect high-rise structures and their occupants. As one source notes (Craighead, 2003, p. 153):

> The primary purpose of a CCTV system is to enhance existing security measures and amplify the range of observation of security staff. To improve security, it may be useful to interface the CCTV system with intercoms and intrusion detection devices such as magnetic door contacts, motion detectors, or video motion detectors. The primary purpose of the video recording system is to record the picture from a camera and provide a permanent record for possible later review. As with other security systems and equipment, such as physical barriers, locking systems, and lighting and intrusion detection systems, CCTV is part of the basic security measures that make up the total security program.

The *Protection of Assets* volume on physical security features a complete discussion of video technology and its application to security. This chapter focuses on camera locations and their monitoring and response capabilities.

Camera locations. Video cameras can be found in the following locations in high-rise structures:

1. *Critical entry or exit areas for pedestrians.* These include the ground level exits from building stairwells, the building perimeter, reception points on critical floors, mechanical floors, and crossover floors between elevator banks. The purpose is to monitor activity and, in the case of the fire stairs, to identify persons who leave the building via the stairwell enclosure.

   Pedestrian access points operated remotely. These include pedestrian doors controlled from a remote location. The camera is needed to help ensure that entry is permitted only to authorized persons, without tailgating or piggybacking occurring.

2. *Access points at which automated access control devices, such as electronic card readers, are featured.* The purpose is to help ensure that only those persons using the card are admitted and that tailgating does not occur.
3. *Inside passenger and service/freight elevator cars.* A camera installed in a visible location inside an elevator may deter threats against persons and property, including vandalism of the elevator itself.
4. *Sensitive interior spaces.* These are any spaces where remote surveillance provides a significant advantage. Such areas include mechanical areas, HVAC air-intakes, vaults, storage areas and elevator lobbies.
5. *Vehicle entrances and exits.* Cameras at entrance and exit points can be used to monitor vehicular activity. For entrances where vehicle access is remotely controlled, a camera can help in determining whether a vehicle should be granted entry. For under-building garages, it is important to record images of all vehicles, including license plates, and the drivers who enter and exit.
6. *Covert surveillance areas.* Cameras can be concealed in a variety of ways and used to monitor and record activity in sensitive locations.[44] However, before they are used, local laws should be checked regarding their legality. Such cameras can be extremely useful in security investigations.

When video cameras are used in conjunction with remote access control, there is also a need for two-way voice communications between persons at the entry and control points.

Monitoring and response. Video surveillance without critical analysis of the activity under observation, or without a response resource if one is needed, is operationally inadequate and economically wasteful.

Surveillance monitoring requires all of the following:

- output from each camera to be displayed at all times unless it can be alarm switched to activate the display when needed
- arrangement of the monitor screens to permit rapid visual analysis by a trained observer
- a means for bringing any particular camera of immediate interest to a monitor screen in the direct field of view of the operator
- the capability for permanently recording the display from one or more cameras, as needed, and for identifying the recorded material by camera location and clock time

---

44 Of course, it is critical that such covert video surveillance not occur in areas where there is an expectation of privacy (such as restrooms, toilets, locker rooms, and changing rooms).

In smaller video systems with two or three cameras, the requirements just noted can be met easily with one monitor for each camera, plus a video recorder. For more elaborate systems, particularly those involving 10 or more cameras, a more sophisticated design is needed. In designing a video system for a high-rise structure, it is important to remember this advice: "Design the application first and fit the equipment to it."[45]

Integrated Security Systems

It is important to have a central location within the high-rise structure where the security systems and equipment can be monitored and controlled. The *Protection of Assets* volume on physical security discusses the design and operation of integrated systems.

If a major integrated system is established, ideally no attempt should be made to use the system control center in any way other than as a dedicated facility. However, due to security staffing and cost considerations, sometimes the control area in a high-rise structure is established in the main lobby or near regularly used entry points. Monitoring personnel are expected to handle both the system demands and the spot demands of persons passing the area. The theoretical savings achieved by requiring that operators attend to other fixed-post duties may cause inattention to system-monitored events of far greater loss consequence. Such an arrangement also exposes the system control to compromise or attack. If the system has been properly designed, ideally the monitoring and control station should be the most secure location in the structure.

Security Personnel

Security personnel are an important aspect of the life safety and security of high-rise structures. Their primary role is to implement the building's life safety and security program. The number of security personnel necessary depends on the type of occupancy and its activities, the objectives of the security and life safety program and the role that security plays in it. For example (Craighead, 2003, p. 267),

> The required levels of staffing for most high-rise office buildings are higher during normal business hours than after hours. During normal business hours, most tenants are open for business and there is an increased population of tenant employees, visitors, salespersons, tradespeople, building management staff, building contractors, couriers, delivery persons, solicitors, building inspectors, and others who may require the attention of building security staff. After hours, pedestrian (and vehicle) traffic usually lessens and only the number of janitorial staff [usually] increases (unless special activities are occurring in the building).

45 Charlie R. Pierce, CPP, in Gips (2001, p. 82).

Policies and Procedures

Clearly defined policies and procedures are an important life safety and security consideration for high-rise structures. Properly documented security instructions—commonly called post orders or standard operating procedures—is an essential reference for security personnel to know what is expected of them. Also, thoroughly documented life safety instructions are a critical component of a building's emergency management plan.

2.4 SUMMARY

Generally, a high-rise structure is considered to be one that extends higher than the maximum reach of available fire-fighting equipment. Such structures have unique life safety and security needs. Since they often contain high concentrations of people and property, they need to be protected against threats that range from fires and natural disasters to criminal activity, including theft of assets, workplace violence, and acts of terrorism.

When certain types of incidents—particularly fires and explosions—occur, it is essential to immediately evacuate occupants to safety. However, due to the limited capacity of building emergency exit stairwells and elevators, not all occupants can leave the facility at once. Therefore, buildings must have up-to-date, thorough, and well-thought-out emergency management plans, and all occupants must be trained to react appropriately if an emergency should occur.

Many security and life safety measures are available to help protect high-rise structures. They must be deployed in a manner that not only meets stringent building and life safety codes but also addresses security needs which vary from structure to structure, depending on its type of tenancy and pattern of use. Sometimes life safety and security considerations conflict with each other; therefore, special consideration must to be given to adequately address life safety requirements without compromising security objectives.

 •

REFERENCES

9/11 Commission report: Final report of the National Commission on Terrorist Attacks Upon the United States (2004). New York: W. W. Norton & Company.

ASIS International Commission on Guidelines (2004). *General security risk assessment guideline.* Alexandria, Virginia: ASIS International.

ASIS International Commission on Guidelines (2004). *Threat advisory system response guideline.* Alexandria, Virginia: ASIS International.

ASIS International Commission on Guidelines (2009). *Facilities physical security measures guideline.* Alexandria, Virginia: ASIS International.

Black's law dictionary, 8th ed. (2004). St. Paul, Minnesota: West Publishing.

Clarke, F. B., PhD (2003). Fire hazards of materials. In A. E. Cote (Ed.), *Fire protection handbook,* 19th ed. Quincy, Massachusetts: National Fire Protection Association.

Craighead, G., CPP (2003 and 2009). *High-rise security and fire life safety,* 2nd and 3rd editions. Burlington, Massachusetts: Elsevier Butterworth-Heinemann.

Donoghue, E. A., CPCA (2003). Building transportation systems. In A. E. Cote (Ed.), *Fire protection handbook,* 19th ed. Quincy, Massachusetts: National Fire Protection Association.

Edgar, J. M., & McInerney, W. D., AHC, CPP (2004). The use of locks in physical crime prevention. In L. J. Fennelly (Ed.), *Handbook of loss prevention and crime prevention,* 4th ed. Stoneham, Massachusetts: Elsevier Butterworth Heinemann. Used with permission of the National Crime Prevention Institute, School of Justice Administration, University of Louisville.

Emergency evacuation elevator systems guideline (2004). Chicago: Council on Tall Buildings and Urban Habitat.

Finneran, E. D. (1981). *Security supervision: A handbook for supervisors and managers.* Stoneham, Massachusetts: Butterworths, 1981. Quoted in L. J. Fennelly (Ed.), *Handbook of loss prevention and crime prevention,* 4th ed. Stoneham, Massachusetts: Elsevier Butterworth Heinemann.

Geringer, R. G. (1991, June). High-rises look to lock out problems. *Access Control,* p. 2.

Gips, M. A. (2001, April). Let's get digital. *Security Management,* p. 82.

Guidance for protecting building environments from airborne chemical, biological, or radiological attacks (2002). Publication No. 2002-139. National Institute for Occupational Safety and Health, Department of Health and Human Services, Centers for Disease Control and Prevention, May 2002, http://www.cdc.gov/niosh.

Hall, J. R., Jr., & Cote, A. E., PE (2003). An overview of the fire problem and fire protection. In A. E. Cote (Ed.), *Fire protection handbook*, 19th ed. Quincy, Massachusetts: National Fire Protection Association.

Healy, R. J. (1983). *Design for security*, 2nd ed. New York: John Wiley & Sons.

Holmes, W. D., PE (2003). Occupancies in special structures and high-rise buildings. In A. E. Cote (Ed.), *Fire protection handbook*, 19th ed. Quincy, Massachusetts: National Fire Protection Association.

Kitteringham, G. W., CPP (2001). A study of two types of vertical crime pattern analysis in the commercial, multi-tenanted high rise structure. Thesis for Master of Science in Security and Crime Risk Management, Scarman Center for the Study of Public Order, Canada, February 2001.

Lathrop, J. K. (2003). Concepts of egress design. In A. E. Cote (Ed.), *Fire protection handbook*, 19th ed. Quincy, Massachusetts: National Fire Protection Association.

Milke, J. A., PhD, PE, & Klote, J. H., DSc, PE (2003). Smoke movement in buildings. In A. E. Cote (Ed.), *Fire protection handbook*, 19th ed. Quincy, Massachusetts: National Fire Protection Association.

Moore, W. D. (2008). Fire alarm systems. In A. E. Cote (Ed.), *Fire protection handbook*, 20th ed. Quincy, Massachusetts: National Fire Protection Association.

National fire code (2001). Quincy, Massachusetts: National Fire Protection Association.

Puchovsky, M. T., PE (2003). Automatic sprinkler systems. In A. E. Cote (Ed.), *Fire protection handbook*, 19th ed. Quincy, Massachusetts: National Fire Protection Association.

Roberts, J. C., PE (2003). Automatic fire detectors. In A. E. Cote (Ed.), *Fire protection handbook*, 19th ed. Quincy, Massachusetts: National Fire Protection Association.

Schifiliti, R. P., PE (2003). Notification appliances. In A. E. Cote (Ed.), *Fire protection handbook*, 19th ed. Quincy, Massachusetts: National Fire Protection Association.

Shapiro, J. M. (2003). Standpipe and hose systems. In A. E. Cote (Ed.), *Fire protection handbook*, 19th ed. Quincy, Massachusetts: National Fire Protection Association.

Taylor, G. M. (2003). Halogenated agents and systems. In A. E. Cote (Ed.), *Fire protection handbook*, 19th ed. Quincy, Massachusetts: National Fire Protection Association.

Webb, W. A., PE (2003). Air-conditioning and ventilating systems. In A. E. Cote (Ed.), *Fire protection handbook*, 19th ed. Quincy, Massachusetts: National Fire Protection Association.

ADDITIONAL SOURCES

Broder, J. F. (2006). *Risk analysis and the security survey*, 3rd ed. Burlington, Massachusetts: Butterworth-Heinemann.

Challinger, Dennis (2008). *From the ground up: security for tall buildings*. CRISP Report Alexandria, Virginia: ASIS International.

Emergency evacuation elevator systems guideline (2004). Chicago: Council on Tall Buildings and Urban Habitat.

Emergency planning guidebook (1994). Washington, DC: Building Owners and Managers Association.

Emergency planning handbook, 2nd ed. (2003). Alexandria, Virginia: ASIS International.

Hopf, P. S. (1979). *Handbook of building security planning and design*. New York: McGraw-Hill.

Kitteringham, Glen, CPP (2006). *Security and fire life safety for the commercial high-rise*. Alexandria, Virginia: ASIS International.

NFPA ready reference: Fire safety in high-rise buildings (2003). Quincy, Massachusetts: NFPA International.

San Luis, E., Tyska, L. A., & Fennelly, L. J. (1994). *Office and office building security*, 2nd ed. Woburn, Massachusetts: Butterworth-Heinemann.

U.S. Marshals Service (1995). *Vulnerability assessment of federal facilities*. Washington, DC: Government Printing Office.

World Trade Center building performance study: Data collection, preliminary observations, and recommendations, (2002). FEMA 403. Washington, DC: Federal Emergency Management Agency.

www.ctbuh.org. The Council on Tall Buildings and Urban Habitat (CTBUH) was established to facilitate professional exchanges among those involved in all aspects of the planning, design, and operation of tall buildings. CTBUH publishes a list of the 100 tallest buildings in the world.

www.emporis.com. This site contains a valuable database of high-rise buildings throughout the world.

CHAPTER 3
MANAGING CORPORATE SPECIAL EVENTS

At a special event, the primary duty of security personnel is to provide safety and security for everyone present. A secondary duty is to safeguard property. To carry out those duties, security professionals can blend security fundamentals with specialized measures appropriate to the unique setting of special events. They will need to develop security plans featuring both preventive and reactive measures, implement the plans well, and manage security staff effectively.

In this context, the terms *special event* and *event* are used interchangeably to designate a public or private assembly. The assembly may occur once, regularly, or daily, and it may be on private property (e.g., hotel or conference center) or public property (e.g., stadium or city street). Events may be entertainment-oriented (sports, business convention festivities) or not (political conventions, demonstrations, funeral processions), and they may include a large or small number of participants. According to the *Rules of the City of New York* (56 R.C.N.Y. §1-02):

> "Special event" means a group activity including, but not limited to, a performance, meeting, assembly, contest, exhibit, ceremony, parade, athletic competition, reading, or picnic involving more than 20 people or a group activity involving less than 20 people for which specific space is requested to be reserved.

3.1 UNIQUE OCCASIONS

Special events present specific circumstances that can challenge the way security personnel plan for the protection of persons and property. Some events are simple, while others are complex spectacles with food, drink, décor, staging, entertainment, lighting, sound, projection equipment, and special effects. Every special event is a unique undertaking, and each venue presents special challenges for security personnel.

No two events are ever the same, even if they have the same name and are held in the same place on a regular basis. For example, an annual shareholder meeting, sales convention, or board meeting can face significantly different security concerns from year to year, depending on factors inside and outside the corporation (such as a poor economy, protest activity, or impending layoffs).

Numerous factors must be considered: location of the event, number of people expected to attend, general makeup of the crowd, ingress and egress, emergency access, etc. An event that is open to the world presents different risks than a fully private, invitation-only event with a small audience.

Despite the differences between specific events, some basic principles apply to various categories of events. For example, the U.S. Occupational Safety and Health Administration promulgates "Crowd Management Safety Guidelines for Retailers" (www.osha.gov/OshDoc/data_General_Facts/Crowd_Control.pdf). The guidelines refer to the 2008 death of a Wal-Mart employee, who died after being knocked to the ground and trampled by a crowd of 2,000 shoppers surging into the store for a "Black Friday" sale.

3.2 SCOPE OF SECURITY RESPONSIBILITIES

The challenge of event security is to protect a wide range of people—the general public, invitees, event and venue personnel, performers, VIPs, volunteers, and service providers—in a way that maintains the hospitality of the event. Overall, the security team's responsibility is to reduce risk.

If an organization is planning an event and its security manager has little experience in event protection, four options arise:

- Do the best one can with current security capabilities.
- Provide personnel with detailed training in special event security issues.
- Hire a special event security provider.
- Accept the risk and provide no security for the event.

Regardless of the choice, someone will be held accountable for any injuries or accidents that could have been foreseen and prevented. The event security environment is particularly sensitive to the need to meet an acceptable standard of care.

Many security professionals who do not primarily deal with event security may find themselves responsible for it occasionally. For example, shopping centers large and small hold special events such as shows, displays, demonstrations, celebrity visits, and concerts. Thus, shopping center security managers may have event security responsibility. The shooting of U.S. Congresswoman Gabrielle Giffords in Tucson, Arizona, on January 8, 2011, shows the consequences of inadequate security planning at a shopping center event. A security professional protecting a special event at a small venue may face many of the same risks as one protecting events at a stadium, convention center, parade, or marathon.

In security planning, it is impossible to identify the scope of responsibility without knowing the risks associated with the event. Without risk assessment, security is reduced to assigning warm bodies here and there at an event site without forethought or strategy. To assess risk, a security professional can use several tools. Here are three examples:

- *Protection of Assets* addresses the concepts underlying risk assessment.
- The Vulnerability Identification Self-Assessment Tool (ViSAT) was developed by the U.S. Department of Homeland Security (DHS) for evaluating the strengths and weaknesses of individual security operations in all types of venues. This online assessment includes more than 200 questions covering seven important areas: security plan, policies, and procedures; security force and security awareness training; cargo, personnel, and vehicle access control; physical security issues; security technology;

communication security; and information security. DHS provides a summary report as well as guidelines for setting priorities for security enhancement. It emphasizes a team approach to security planning.

- DHS's Risk Self-Assessment Tool (RSAT) is a Web-based application designed to help managers of stadiums and arenas identify and manage security vulnerabilities.

In terms of staff, for each event a single person should be designated as the event security director, the person at whose desk the buck stops. That person is responsible for the overall design of the security plan, its implementation, and management of security personnel. Once defined, the security scope dictates the duties of security personnel. Every security member must be familiar with the overall security plan and understand where he or she fits in.

Some events may require one security officer or contracted company to provide security planning, personnel, and equipment, while other events involve many security personnel and numerous organizations. Events may also include different types of law enforcement agencies: city, county, state, and federal. The 2010 Winter Olympic Games in Vancouver, Canada, were protected by police officers from across the country, as well as the Canadian armed forces.

Most federal, state, and municipal laws do not specify private security responsibilities for special events, other than licensing and basic security training, screening, and firearms requirements. However, a jurisdiction may require certain security measures from an event planner seeking a permit to hold an event on public property.

3.3 FACTORS IN EVENT PLANNING

In planning security for a special event, the objective is to maintain a safe and secure environment and to deal with interruptions or emergencies quickly, in a way that allows the event to continue and minimizes the effects of the emergency. The following factors directly affect the design and implementation of the security plan. The security planner should anticipate circumstances related to these factors to foresee difficulties or breakdowns that may arise in implementing the security plan.

3.3.1 TIME-SENSITIVITY

Security personnel must be ready for the crowd's arrival, even if others involved in the event are not ready. Security personnel must also be ready to handle constant changes in the environment. Sometimes VIP guests are included at the last minute, designated parking areas are changed, entrance and exit patterns are modified, one event activity is exchanged for another, crowd movement corridors are modified, or activities are added to an event. Security must be prepared for appropriate contingencies.

3.3.2 ORGANIZATIONAL STRUCTURE

Accidents and incidents often result from misunderstanding of responsibilities by event organizers, facility managers, or security personnel. Such misunderstandings may be caused by a lack of a clear organizational chain of command, inexperienced personnel, lack of adequate training, contractual agreements, poor communication, or lack of written policies and procedures. A good, clear organizational structure can minimize misunderstandings.

3.3.3 VOLUNTEERS

It is difficult to manage and coordinate large numbers of part-time volunteers, who may have a lot of enthusiasm but no experience. While they can be helpful, they should clearly understand the limits of their duties and know how to contact the correct personnel to resolve issues.

3.3.4 LOCATION

Many events are held in facilities or venues designed for crowds and events (stadiums, arenas, convention centers, concert halls). Basic operations plans that are easily modified for each event are already established and documented. These locations already have clearly designated entry and exit access areas, plenty of well-distributed restrooms, clear directional signage, crowd control and access barriers, medical facilities, command or operations centers, parking and traffic controls, and video surveillance equipment.

Some events take place in unusual locations not specifically designed for crowds. These temporary event sites may create security and safety problems related to seating arrangements, crowd movement, restroom facilities, parking and traffic, emergency access, evacuation, and placement of equipment. Security must always request the most recent event site maps, showing how the site will be laid out before and during the event. Security must assess the configuration and suggest any necessary changes based on security and safety concerns.

3.3.5 CROWDS, PARTICIPANTS, AND ATTENDEES

One concern is that events may attract an over-capacity crowd. As the number of people increases, so does the probability of accidents and incidents. For larger crowds, additional security precautions and security personnel may be required for traffic control, parking, admission and access control points, and concessions. It is not always easy for an event security director to determine the number of people anticipated. Therefore, contingency planning is critical.

Security must also know how many event personnel are involved. An event may feature service providers for setting up scaffolding, fences, musical equipment, signs, and decorations. In the early stages of event planning, only a few people may be involved, but many more (hundreds or thousands) may join in closer to the event's starting time.

A critical factor is to know the audience. Security personnel have different concerns depending on the average age of the audience, how many small children or senior citizens may be present, and whether wheelchair patrons are expected. Some events attract demonstrators or others who use the event to gain publicity or commit crimes. Law enforcement agencies are a valuable source of information on such groups.

Some events involve foreign attendees who do not understand the local language, are not accustomed to local social practices, or do not know local laws. They may not be able to read safety or security signs or understand spoken instructions. Public announcements—especially for emergency and evacuation circumstances—should be prepared in the languages of the anticipated audience.

Crowds raise parking and traffic flow concerns. The security team should consider designated vehicle traffic flow at ingress and egress points as well as pedestrian traffic flow through parking lots and approaches to the event. Clear parking and traffic signage is essential. Portable traffic barriers make it possible to change routes as traffic flow changes or for emergency evacuation.

3.3.6 TYPE OF EVENT

The general nature of the event will likely suggest an approach to security. The event may be artistic, musical, sporting, political, cause-related, civic, community-oriented, or religious. Within each category, differences between particular events may further influence security planning. For example, a heavy metal concert presents different risks than a church choir concert. Sporting events might present different risks depending on the particular sport, team rivalries, importance of the game, and venue (indoors or outdoors).

The security plan must also consider the numerous secondary activities associated with the primary activity. The primary activity of a marathon is the race itself, yet the event may encompass many secondary activities, such as concerts, concessions, display booths, fund-raising or cause-related activities, children's activities, and political presentations.

Many events feature circumstances that have no exact precedent. An event might have been marketed extensively, might be scheduled to last for several days or weeks, or might host political leaders, celebrities, or controversial figures. For any of those circumstances, the effects are hard to predict.

3.3.7 COMMUNICATION

Security coordination during the event requires clear communication for both normal operations and unexpected occurrences. At small events, staff may be in sight of each other. For large events a command center, operations center, or both may be needed. Depending on the type of event, it may be necessary to establish a communication link with government or other organizations.

Electronic communication may be affected by the terrain or size of the venue. Security, medical, and fire personnel are often seen using two-way radio communication, yet other communication equipment is important at some events, such as cell phones, electronic message boards, scoreboards, electronic public address boards, televisions, and bullhorns. Security staff should ensure that all communication equipment is tested and in full working condition before the event. They should also have a clear understanding of the policies and procedures for using communication equipment during normal event operations and emergencies.

The security plan should also address media locations (rooms for computers and telephones and sites for fixed and mobile television cameras), policies for press tags and credentials, access control, screening and searches, and protocols for media interviews and requests.

3.3.8 WEATHER

Weather can affect both indoor and outdoor events. Attention should be given to heat, rain, hail, snow, ice, and weather extremes, any of which could affect audience well-being and increase the risks in parking and traffic control. Different weather calls for different security equipment, tools, machinery, and vehicles.

3.3.9 BUDGET

A complete security plan should include a proposed budget for event security. The overall event planners may view security as holding secondary importance, yet an inadequate security budget could turn an award-winning event into a disaster. The actual budget should be based on the planning committee's decision to accept, transfer, or avoid risk.

3.4 COMPONENTS OF A SPECIAL EVENT SECURITY PLAN

The preceding considerations should culminate in a comprehensive security plan. A well-documented plan allows for the efficient implementation of security measures. The appendix presents an event security plan outline. Because the plan will likely change during the planning process, it is important to date each page of the document and discard old versions to avoid confusion. For security purposes, it may be wise to provide complete copies to a limited number of people and to provide others with only those portions applicable to them. The security plan for a small event may be brief, while one for a large event may include even more topics than those suggested below.

- **Mission statement.** The mission statement should very simply describe what the security operation is tasked with doing. For example, the mission may be to provide comprehensive security and safety to all for the concert in the park. The statement could be expanded, but it clearly defines the purpose.

- **Scope.** The scope of security's responsibility (the *what* and *how*) should be defined to include logistical scope as well as delineated duties, such as access control and parking patrol.

- **Security plan site maps.** The plan should also include current site maps that reflect as much information as necessary for security personnel to complete their assignments.

- **Security and liaison personnel.** The personnel section of the special event security plan includes the chain of command as well as event contacts and government agency liaisons. The event security director should consider providing pocket-sized copies of this section.

- **Command or operations center.** In this section the plan identifies the incident command center or operations center, which will serve as an information and response hub at the event site. The center provides a central location from which to direct operations, monitor the event site, and handle responses to emergencies and non-emergencies. Depending on the nature of the event, it may make sense to establish a principal command center with multiple field centers in different locations. Mobile command centers may also prove useful.

  The center should be in a location that is protected as much as possible from all weather conditions, including severe storms and flooding. The center should have only the minimum number of access points required for efficient operations. Access should be restricted to personnel who have duties in the center.

  Inside the center should be representatives from various departments and organizations: the event-hosting organization, facility management, law enforcement agencies, security department, fire marshal, medical director, sponsors, promoters, transportation and parking, and accommodations. Primary representatives in the center must have a backup in case a field post is established during an emergency. Additional information can be found in the *Protection of Assets* volume on crisis management.

- **Access control and searches.** Access control is a way of screening who may enter a given area and under what conditions (e.g., with a ticket or credential). *Admissions control* refers to the control of items or objects not allowed into the event area (such guns, fireworks, alcohol, chains, knives, ice chests, bottles, cans, cameras, nails, or screws). The plan should call for a clearly designated event site perimeter and establish policies and procedures for controlling and securing it.

  At some events, searches at the admission gate may be required. At a 2001 University of Oklahoma home football game against Kansas State, with a crowd of 84,000 packed into Memorial Stadium, a bomb detonated outside the site. The alleged bomber reportedly had tried to enter the stadium but ran away when he saw that his backpack would be searched.

  The event security plan should specify such points as the following:

  — Searches and screeners must receive adequate, documented training and clear, written procedures based on legal advice.

  — All persons attempting to enter must be treated equally.

  — Understandable, easy-to-read signage must identify what items searchers will look for. The signs should be placed at all public and employee entrances, in parking areas, and along walkways from the parking lots to the event entrances. Signage should state a person's options if he or she chooses not to be searched. That information should also be placed on tickets, brochures, and programs.

  — If pat-down searches will be conducted, patrons should be given plenty of notice and informed why such procedures are in place. They should also be informed that if they do not consent to the search, they may not enter. (Legal advice may be needed before conducting searches at government-owned facilities.)

  — If metal detectors and X-ray machines are used, an appropriate number of machines and trained operators must be assured.

  — If a person sets off the alarm on a metal detector, there should be a second metal detector in the immediate vicinity available for a second detection.

  — If people are free to come and go from an event site, then a search must be performed each time they return.

  — Only males should search males, and only females should search females.

  — Each individual should be asked for permission for the search.

- **Emergency response.** Security staff may well be the first responders to an on-site emergency. They might have to deal with medical concerns, fire, hazardous materials, water and sewer line breaks, inclement weather, earthquakes, failures of communications or utilities, failure of key suppliers, explosions, civil unrest or disturbance, strikes, kidnappings, or terrorism. The security plan should address contingencies and attach specific instructions for responding to each, including evacuation plans.

Designing an event security plan involves much more than assigning the locations and hours of security officers. Experienced event security professionals know that each event requires detailed, custom planning that considers a great array of factors. Fortunately, a combination of basic security strategies, distinctive security measures for special events, and risk assessment tools can provide the framework for a safe and secure event.

APPENDIX A

MODEL EVENT SECURITY PLAN

EVENT SECURITY PLAN

for

[Name of event]
[Date of event]
[Location of event]

This is a strictly confidential document to be used by the director of event security. Only [name of the director of event security or others] may approve, with written and signed permission, any copying or distribution of this document.

Section 1: Mission Statement

Example: It is our mission to provide for the on-site security and safety of all people involved in this event's operations and attendance as designated by contract (if applicable). We are committed to providing competent, courteous, professional, and effective service. We will exercise reasonable care in reducing the severity of risk to life and damage to property under our control. To this end we will establish total manpower needs before, during, and after all event activities (as specified by contract) for the protection of people, property, privileged information, and all other assets. (Include a copy of the signed agreement in the appendix. Number the pages.)

[Each page should be dated and should be numbered as page 2 of 25, 3 of 25, and so on.]

Section 2: Scope

Example: The scope of the responsibilities of [name of company or individual] in this security plan is limited to providing [parking lot security, VIP security, stage security, concession area security, or other].

Alternate example: The scope of the responsibilities in this security plan includes all aspects of the event. All security agencies and organizations, both public and private, are included in this security plan.

2-A. Security Planning Team

The following individuals have been designated as the decision makers in the planning of security at this event:

Name	Title	Agency/Company	Telephone Number

2-B. Event Description

Here one includes or attaches the most current or final

- brochures,
- programs, or
- media information.

Section 3: Event Site Diagram and Map of Vicinity

Here one includes or attaches the most current or final

- event site map,
- facility or venue map if not the same,
- local neighborhood street map indicating locations of hospitals, police departments, fire stations, vacant lots, off-site parking lots, liquor stores, construction zones, parks, schools, and other relevant features, and
- in foreign countries, maps of the greater area, noting bridges, rivers, embassies, and hotels.

Section 4: Security and Liaison Personnel

4-A. General Company or Agency Description

Here one includes or attaches a description of all the specific types of security or law enforcement personnel with the number of each, the names of the organizations, contact persons, and telephone numbers. These may not be the on-site personnel for the event. The list should include the following:

- the facility's in-house security personnel
- contracted outside security personnel
- municipal law enforcement
- county law enforcement
- highway patrol and state police
- federal agencies: U.S. Secret Service, FBI, Bureau of Alcohol, Tobacco, Firearms, and Explosives, and Immigration and Customs Enforcement
- military police or personnel used as security officers
- any foreign security or police personnel with responsibilities relevant to the event

4-B. Effective On-site Liaison

Each internal or external entity involved in the operation of the event must provide the name of a final decision maker for its segment of the operation. An alternate must also be named. Both landline and mobile telephone numbers are needed. In case of a question while the event is in progress, the decision maker must be immediately available. These decision makers include representatives of fire departments, medical facilities, emergency management agencies, and, if the event is held in a foreign country, U.S. State Department officials.

4-C. On-Site Chain of Command

Perhaps the most important item relating to the implementation of the security plan and management of all security personnel, especially for large events, is an agreed chain of command for security operations.

4-D. Operations/Command Center Personnel

This is a list of all personnel who will be authorized to enter the operations or command center.

4-E. Legal Compliance

All security personnel must be in full compliance with all applicable laws and regulations.

4-F. Security Company Documentation

If a contingent work force is used to provide security, each entity should provide a statement documenting the laws to which it is subject regarding the security service it will provide. Documentation also includes operations manuals, policies and procedures, rules and regulations, training manuals and workbooks, and event handouts.

Section 5: Communication

Security staff must review the overall event communication plan from a security perspective and make appropriate recommendations. Security communication must be able to tie into the entire event's communication system. The event security plan should address the following items:

- assessment of security communication requirements at fixed posts as well as for patrolling or roving security
- assessment of fire, medical, and emergency communication requirements
- need for collar microphones, headsets, and earpieces
- storage, installation, recharging, and repair of equipment
- user instructions and training
- distribution policies and procedures
- radio frequency channel assignments
- pre-event testing
- backup systems
- protection and security of communication equipment
- command post or operations center
- Federal Communication Commission regulations
- testing of all communication equipment

Section 6: Event Schedule and Timeline

The event schedule and timeline should provide an overall calendar of everything that will take place in preparation for the event, during the event, and after the event. It should note the timing of the following:

- planning sessions and countdown meetings
- training
- event briefing
- sign-in and issuance of equipment
- setup
- delivery of supplies and materials
- mounting of signs
- beginning of traffic control
- opening of parking areas
- start of admissions
- opening of concessions
- beginning of event
- major crowd movements to anticipate
- intermissions
- relocation of security
- VIP protection
- closing of concessions
- end of primary event activity or entertainment
- end of other event activities
- closing of parking lot
- collection of equipment
- debriefing sessions
- sign-out
- lockup
- teardown
- cleanup
- after-hours security
- payment of security personnel

Section 7: Security Post Assignments

Post assignments are the specific locations and job descriptions given to each security officer. Each should know exactly what to do at the particular location, especially when reassigned to a different position as required by the schedule of activities. Duties change from one place to another. A job description should not be lengthy (unless necessary) and may consist of two or three particular duties. Common post assignments include the following:

- command and operations centers
- perimeter areas: fences, walls, natural boundaries, barricades, etc.
- traffic control areas: streets and intersections
- parking areas for the public, staff, handicapped patrons, VIPs, deliveries, etc.
- bus loading and unloading zones
- ticket sales and entrance zones

- admission areas for the public, personnel, volunteers, VIPs, deliveries, emergency services, etc.
- general public areas: hallways, doorways, aisles, concessions, restrooms, etc.
- restricted access areas: backstage, stages, administrative offices, storage areas, garages, media and press zones, medical stations, ticket offices, lost and found, etc.
- roving teams
- special teams: bicycle, motorcycle, horse, and boat patrols
- cash collection teams
- undercover or plainclothes security
- sleeping quarters for event personnel, performers, participants, etc.
- overnight security

Section 8: Security Equipment

A security team must be properly equipped to complete its mission. Putting equipment requirements on paper requires one to think about what is needed, what is missing, and what the costs might be. Categories of security equipment include the following:

- signage
- access control equipment: barriers, barricades, stanchions, rope, fencing, etc.
- search equipment: metal detectors (walk-through and handheld), gloves, etc.
- communication equipment
- vehicles: automobiles, bicycles, golf carts, motorcycles, boats, snowmobiles, horses, Segways, etc.
- weapons
- uniforms and other personal attire
- other gear: flashlights, clipboards, metal detectors, hats, helmets, handcuffs, cameras, evidence tags, binoculars, incident reports, pens, pencils, etc.
- on-site office equipment: computers, printers, office supplies, etc.

Section 9: Emergency Response Procedures

Security staff may encounter various types of emergencies. Each security officer must be trained in the policies and procedures regarding the following:

- incident and accident reports and documentation
- security response to fires
- security response to injuries
- emergency response
- evacuation
- media and public relations issues

Section 10: Post-Event Conference

A post-event conference should be held to review all facets of the event operation and all actions taken in the course of the event.

Section 11: Attachments

The event security plan should include the following as attachments:

- all risk assessment reports and conclusions:
  — from private security consultants
  — from any law enforcement agency or government office
  — from the Vulnerability Identification Self-Assessment Tool (ViSAT)
  — from the Risk Self-Assessment Tool (RSAT)
- security intelligence reports of vulnerabilities and threats
- fire marshal inspections
- site inspections
- disaster plan
- mass arrest plan
- bomb squad plan
- demonstration or protester plan
- dignitary and VIP plan

ADDITIONAL READING

Bellavita, C. (2007). Changing homeland security: A strategic logic of special event security. *Homeland Security Affairs* [Online], v. III, no. 3. *Crowd Management Magazine*, International Association of Assembly Managers (IAAM).

Facility Manager [bimonthly], [Online]. (2006, October to date). Coppell, TX: International Association of Venue Managers, Inc. Available: http://www.iavm.org/facility_manager/pages/facility_issues.htm [2011, October 14].

Facility Manager [bimonthly]. Coppell, TX; International Association of Venue Managers, Inc.

International Association of Venue Managers. (1998). *IAAM crowd management curriculum project report* [Online]. Available: http://www.iavm.org/cvms/crowd_management.asp [2011, October 14].

Journal of Crowd Safety & Security Management [irregular], [Online]. (2009 to date). International Centre for Crowd Management and Bucks New University. Available: http://www.crowdsafetymanagement.co.uk/journal [2011, October 14].

Journal of Convention and Event Tourism [quarterly]. Binghamton, NY: Haworth Press.

Public Risk Magazine [10x year]. Arlington, VA: Public Risk and Insurance Management Association (PRIMA).

Public Venue Security [Online]. (2003, Sept/Oct, to 2004, March/April). Phoenix, AZ: Virgo Publishing. Available: http://www.publicvenuesecurity.com/archives.html [2011, October 14].

Risk Management Magazine [monthly], [Online]. (2003 to date). New York, NY: The Risk Management Society. Available: http://www.rmmag.com/MGTemplate.cfm?section=MagArchive&Template=/Magazine/ArchivedMagazines.cfm [2011, October 14].

Risk Management Magazine [monthly]. New York, NY: The Risk Management Society.

Security Management [monthly], [Online]. (2004, June, to date). Alexandria, VA: ASIS International. Available: http://securitymanagement.com. [2011, October 14].

Security Management [monthly]. Alexandria, VA: ASIS International.

Venue Safety & Security [irregular], [Online]. (2007, Summer, to 2010, May). Boise, ID: International Festival and Events Association. Available: http://www.ifea.com/joomla1_5/index.php?option=com_content&view=article&id=112&Itemid=62 [2011, October 14].

CHAPTER 4
SECURITY IN A GLOBAL ENVIRONMENT

The ever-changing global economy presents unique challenges for the security practitioner. Operations abroad represent a significant investment to any organization. Often the practitioner must act as a holistic risk manager, constantly monitoring, evaluating, and adjusting as needed. Security practitioners must be fully cognizant of the proper levels of support for the protection of people, process, assets, and information wherever they reside or traverse.

In 2005, Thomas Friedman's bestseller *The World Is Flat* described increased opportunities for outsourcing business operations to offshore destinations using rapidly advancing technology. Western business operations migrated to the developing world, and formerly small economies were invigorated by the business opportunities and became new consumers for global products and services.

With this quick growth of business in a global environment, additional security risk issues began to present themselves. The advent of social networking and other technologies influences the risk landscape, both positively and negatively, every day. Such risks affect an enterprise's personnel, reputation, operation, and profitability.

Emergency and continuity planning must be incorporated into any global security approach. As the fluidity of worldwide geopolitical risk continues, practitioners must anticipate issues and have plans to safeguard personnel while ensuring continuity of operations. Security planning must consider local laws and cultures, as well as any bias on the security practitioner's part.

Foreign operations and business assignments bring different and sometimes greater risks than domestic operations. If the enterprise is to succeed, it must analyze the risk of each activity and decide whether to accept, mitigate, or transfer that risk.

4.1 POLICIES AND GUIDELINES FOR INTERNATIONAL SECURITY OPERATIONS

4.1.1 WHO SHOULD BE COVERED?

Entities should develop policies and guidelines that apply to personnel who undertake international business travel or assignments on their behalf. These policies may apply to company personnel worldwide, irrespective of home or host location, or they may be tailored for specific locations and situations. Many organizations use contractors on foreign assignments, and care must be taken to understand expectations for their security. In some cases, the organization may wish to include such contractors in their international protection program.

The policies and guidelines should address security for at least these categories of persons:

- *employees:* both full and part-time
- *expatriates:* employees temporarily residing or working in another country
- *local national employees:* employees who are permanent residents of the country they are working in (when the organization is based in another country)
- *contractors:* persons who work for a firm that contracts with the organization, or persons who work directly for the organization under a personal services or employment contract

4.1.2 PURPOSE OF THE POLICIES AND GUIDELINES

Policies and guidelines outline the guiding principles and general terms and conditions that apply to security for personnel travel or international living arrangements.

The policies and guidelines attempt to

- provide the company with the appropriate information to assess business and personal risks associated with specific countries,
- provide personnel with the appropriate tools and methods to reduce those risks, and
- reduce the risk of loss of company personnel and other assets.

International travel and work assignments bring additional risks that are different from those found in domestic operations. Both the employee and employer should be aware of those risks and make decisions based on the ability to implement appropriate countermeasures. International work also requires a high degree of sensitivity to, and respect for, foreign cultures and laws.

Expectations of both the organization and the employee (or contractor) should be fully explored and defined. For example, employees hurt on a weekend sightseeing excursion should understand each party's responsibilities in advance.

International security applications should be guided by the following tenets:

- **Organization's core values and beliefs.** Integrity, high standards, and industry leadership should be maintained in international business.
- **Risk analysis.** The organization and its employees, contractors, and family members should understand the nature and extent of the risks involved in international travel and employee assignments. This tenet involves the *duty of care* and *duty to disclose*, as described in the *Travel Risk Management Maturity Model* (iJet Intelligent Risk Systems, 2009).
- **Acceptable levels of risk.** Appropriate countermeasures should be in place to reduce the risk to an acceptable level. This step is referred to as the *standard of care* (iJet Intelligent Risk Systems, 2009).
- **Personal responsibility for safety.** Employees, contractors, and family members should implement these standards to ensure that travel and assignments are carried out safely and securely. This is commonly referred to as the *duty to comply*.
- **Responsibility for protecting the organization's assets.** Employees should take appropriate measures to protect the organization's assets, including people, property, information, and stakeholder relationships.
- **Responsibility for protecting the organization's reputation.** Employees and those working directly with the organization should support and maintain its reputation.
- **Compliance with laws and customs.** Employees should respect and comply with home and host country laws, regulations, customs, and business norms. This, too, is part of the duty to comply.

4.2 ACCOUNTABILITIES AND RESPONSIBILITIES

The following subsections state key accountabilities and responsibilities of various parties in the organization:

Business Leader

- Ensure that employees and contractors on international assignments are aware of security requirements.
- Help them meet those requirements.
- Ensure appropriate crisis response.
- Assess communications requirements for the assignment, including contact and protection of confidential proprietary information.

Human Capital Leader

- Ensure that employees are covered by the appropriate insurance, including travel, medical, and evacuation (medical/security) insurance.
- Ensure that personal profiles, including baseline medical information, are maintained.
- Establish a process and expectations regarding travel policy.

Travel Leader

- Ensure that employees understand the support available and conduct expected through an extensive policy.
- Champion a travel policy that empowers travelers to be responsible and accountable for their actions in exigent situations.

Security Leader

- Assist with sensitive issues affecting business operations, such as employee background investigation for joint ventures, assessment of corrupt practices in the culture, extreme weather, etc.
- Provide risk assessments for route of travel, medical concerns, ground transportation, hotel, etc.
- Provide stewardship for an international crisis management plan and prepare for foreseeable events.
- Ensure that travelers have access to the appropriate tools and resources to assess risks and receive country-specific advice in real time.

International Traveler

- Obtain and review risk assessments.
- Take appropriate action to protect the traveler and the company from physical harm and harm to reputation.
- Report any incident, loss, or condition that may cause risk to the traveler.
- Monitor and report any events that may change the level of risk during the course of the assignment.

4.3 COUNTRY RISK CATEGORIES

Various methodologies are used to determine a risk rating; there is no global standard for rating risk. Some analysts use a simple "low, medium, high" rating while others employ a multi-level numeric rating system. When using a private service that rates risk in a city, country, or region, it is important to study the components that lead to that rating. These services scour open-source media and official government reports, and they often employ persons on the ground to track developments and craft timely ratings. However, they do not operate from a common baseline.

Additionally, government organizations like the U.S. Department of State (especially its Overseas Security Advisory Council, www.osac.gov), the British Foreign and Commonwealth Office (www.fco.gov.uk), and others supply useful reports and advice. While these organizations do not rate risks, they do issue warnings and recommendations as situations dictate. In fact, the U.S. Department of State sells a smart phone application for warnings.

The security manager should have access to suppliers who can provide risk assessments on the countries of destination. The assessment of risk may also be based on the nature of corporate activities, including the expected public reaction to the endeavor and any incident history from the organization's own activities in the country. Other multinational companies working in the area may also be a source of information on risk trends and benchmark countermeasures. The organization's staff overseas may be able to offer relevant insights, as well.

Services operate in both pull and push delivery models. Under the pull methodology, the user must proceed to a Web site and actively search data for a country or region. Under the push methodology, systems can be automated to interface with an airline itinerary, a facility location, or other factors to robotically dispatch changes in the risk rating or information of interest to a user. These services can provide virtually real-time information to a traveler or expatriate.

The level of risk is assessed based on country reports developed by the security department or received from security consultants assigned to conduct the review. Risks may change over time and should be updated on a regular basis. A high-risk rating will not automatically mean an arbitrary cancellation of travel to that country, but it will serve as a reminder of the need for appropriate countermeasures.

Risk ratings are continually monitored and adjusted for change by all organizations. Technology allows for easy access by both organizations and travelers in transit.

The following are characteristics of countries with various risk ratings:

Low Risk

- advanced communications
- well-trained medical practitioners
- modern and well-equipped medical facilities
- reliable law enforcement and military
- stable government with a high degree of continuity or change through due process
- no arbitrary treatment of business or travelers by government or the legal system
- controlled crime rates
- history of civil rights

Medium Risk

- communication network that is unreliable or subject to breakdown
- high ratio of poorly trained medical practitioners
- restricted medical supplies and facilities
- history of high crime rates or terrorist activities in some areas of the country
- history of travel disruption
- some lack of control of criminal or terrorist elements by the government of that country
- weak economy
- unreliable law enforcement or military
- history of rebellion or overthrow of the government
- short-term political security but no long-term guarantee
- lack of due process

High Risk

- extensive history of crime or terrorism and a history of threats against foreign nationals
- poorly trained medical practitioners
- restricted medical supplies and facilities
- political, economic, and legal institutions that are highly vulnerable or have ceased to function
- recent or long-term insurgency and political unrest
- violent factions within the country or existence of war or civil war
- law enforcement or military that is either nonexistent or unable to control crime or terrorism
- history of travel advisories from reputable sources
- little or no protection for foreign travelers

Risk assessments are based on the severity of the risk and the likelihood of the occurrence.

4.4 RATING IMPACT ON THE TRAVELER

Personnel who will be traveling internationally on business should take the following steps, based on the assessed risk level:

Low Risk

- Comply with air travel policy, including charter requirements.
- Report incidents and accidents, including threats.
- File a personal profile.

Medium Risk

- Take all the steps above.
- Undergo a baseline medical exam.
- Obtain a travel health assessment.
- Assess communications capability in the country of destination before travel.
- Obtain first aid training.
- Carry an emergency medical kit.

- Carry a vehicle emergency medical kit if road travel is extensive.
- Contact the embassy or consulate at the country of destination.
- Use a local security consultant.
- Use a local driver for transportation.
- Obtain advice on physical security for accommodation.
- Take security awareness training.

High Risk

- Take all the steps above.
- Take a satellite telephone if appropriate.

4.5 PERSONNEL LIVING ABROAD

Employees or contractors who will be living in a foreign country for an extended period may wish to consider the following steps:

Low Risk

- Obtain media training (employees only).
- File a personal profile (for employee and each accompanying family member).

Medium Risk

- Take all the steps above.
- Register with the embassy or consulate at the country of destination.
- Obtain a risk assessment on any proposed accommodation and office or operating site.
- Obtain a travel health assessment for each person traveling.

High Risk

- Take all the steps above.
- Obtain first aid training for each person traveling (children excepted).

4.6 RISKS THAT MAY BE ENCOUNTERED

Foreign travel and operations introduce a number of risks to the organization. The security practitioner is ideally situated to identify risks through analysis and to identify countermeasures to help manage those risks.

4.6.1 CRIME

Crime is one of the most common risks for the foreign traveler. A foreigner in a developing or disrupted country has a high profile and perceived wealth. Further, a lack of understanding of the foreign legal system and language, coupled with the need to maintain a business schedule, makes the traveler a target of opportunity. It is common for criminals to frequent upscale hotels and restaurants or to employ operatives within the staff as criminal accomplices (sometimes incapacitating victims with drugs or alcohol).

Carjacking and "tiger kidnappings" have become prevalent in some countries. These activities usually are an effort to obtain quick cash or valuables from a traveler. Security awareness is helpful, as is maintaining a low profile in terms of dress and vehicle.

Crime types and levels vary from one country to another. In some countries the justice system is almost nonexistent and foreigners are at high risk. A company awareness program should teach traveling employees to deal with that risk by avoiding situations that place them in jeopardy. Employees must learn to be streetwise in foreign locations to avoid violence and local cons. Employees should also be given tools to deal with a criminal confrontation or robbery.

Women may be especially vulnerable in cultures that do not readily accept their participation in business. Sexual harassment and assaults may occur in these environments. Countermeasures such as secured transportation and the "buddy rule" should be employed.

4.6.2 ARREST AND INCARCERATION

Occasionally travelers are not aware of local customs or law and are arrested by local authorities for an action they did not recognize as a violation. Authorities may hold a traveler's passport until some action is taken (such as signing a contract). Travelers must remain calm and ask for assistance from their country's diplomatic representation.

4.6.3 ILLNESS

Many countries lack appropriate medical supplies, trained medical practitioners, or adequate medical facilities. The security manager should ensure that travelers understand the local medical delivery system, including emergency transportation and specialized techniques. For instance, an employee deployed to a remote location in the developing world who has a pre-existing heart condition should be aware of the risk of not receiving treatment during the "golden minutes" (the period when medical treatment has the highest likelihood of preventing death).

Organizations may elect to use private suppliers of medical assistance and evacuation, some of which bundle country risk ratings with their services. These firms can help travelers find proper medical care in-country and evacuate them if necessary. Additionally, these firms can give medical advice by phone when a traveler needs a high-level diagnosis and possible referral.

Travelers from developed countries are used to proficient medical evacuation services, such as ambulance, air ambulance, and emergency response teams. These services are not readily available in developing countries, nor are hospitals and clinics. One response is to equip employees with a robust medical kit and first aid training so they can treat themselves and others.

4.6.4 ACCIDENT

Traffic accidents pose a threat to travelers, especially in countries lacking controlled movement. Road and traffic ratings are available from private and government sources.

4.6.5 NATURAL DISASTER

In the developed world, many companies expect help from first responders in case of a natural disaster. Recent world events have demonstrated that in a major event responders are overwhelmed. In the developing world, the impact of disasters is multiplied by the minimal response. In the early days of an event there, a business traveler and facility manager will need to be self-sufficient, acting without government support.

4.6.6 GEOPOLITICAL EVENTS

Challenges to local government may sweep up business travelers and local national employees in their whirlwind. These events may also affect the business facility or it supply chain.

4.7 COUNTERMEASURES

Countermeasures take several forms and may be part of either a global or a localized approach, depending on the situation.

4.7.1 GENERAL INTELLIGENCE BRIEFINGS

Travelers to foreign destinations need knowledge of the environments they will traverse or be operating in. Organizations should give employees general information on security, safety, and comfort before they depart. These briefings can address ground transport, watercraft, food and water safety, severe weather, and other travel issues, as well as criminal and terror threats in the country or region.

4.7.2 THREAT-SPECIFIC BRIEFINGS

Travelers also need specific information on emerging threats and some knowledge of threat history. For instance, many terror groups' new activities are timed to match key anniversaries. Various private firms monitor open and back-channel sources, anniversary dates, and current activities and can share that information with the organization or its travelers.

4.7.3 INTELLIGENCE FORECASTS

These forecasts, usually created at the country and region level, can be used before investing in a business activity. Generally these forecasts address anticipated security risks and cultural and geopolitical issues.

4.7.4 CONTINGENCY AND EVACUATION PLANNING

Contingency plans must provide for a response to increased risk or a specific event, and they should clarify responsibilities during and after an event. To train, the emergency response group should conduct contingency exercises. The corporate communications group should also consider a crisis communications plan to deal with press and publicity in case of a major event.

The corporate contingency plan should set up a corporate emergency response team and include an international emergency plan that addresses medical emergencies, criminal threats, and evacuation. Most plans include three stages: an alert stage, a preparation-for-evacuation stage, and an evacuation stage. The plan should also include stand-fast procedures in case it is not safe to move employees or their families out of the country.

Where there is a chance of severe natural disaster or civil or political disruption, the employer should prepare an evacuation plan with the following elements:

- **Policy statement.** This is a statement of the organization's commitment to the protection of its employees and a requirement for employees to take personal precautions.
- **General security requirements for office, vehicle, and home.** Employees may need to stock provisions, passports, other essential documents, emergency cash, etc. Communications procedures and callout capabilities for radio or satellite telephone should addressed, as should vehicle security and physical security for the home.
- **Crisis management team.** The crisis management team may include a local team in the foreign country and a corporate team to manage the crisis from home. The plan should include the responsibilities and roles of each team member.
- **Alert levels.** Alert levels often include a monitoring level, where there are indications that the level of risk to personnel is increasing; a "stand-by for information" level; an evacuation level, where steps are taken to remove personnel from the country; and a stand-fast level when conditions are too dangerous to undertake an evacuation.
- **Action plans.** Action plans for all alert levels should include a check list for each team member, outlining actions required during an emergency. Plans should also outline evacuation options for the various types of emergencies, as well as possible suppliers.

4.7.5 COMMUNICATIONS

While the world is more connected each day because of technology, challenges still exist. Some areas have no phone coverage at all, while other use systems that are incompatible with travelers' cell phones from home. Another challenge is knowing the dialing protocols in different countries. In some cases satellite phones may be needed. Security leaders must ensure that travelers have appropriate technology and know how to operate it.

4.8 MEDICAL CONSIDERATIONS

International travel provides a number of medical risks, and the quality of medical services varies. Ambulance service may be rudimentary. Many countries have well-trained medical practitioners but limited access to medical supplies. Employers can minimize medical risk with precautions such as first aid training, medical kits, vaccinations, travel insurance, and evacuation plans. In some cases, the precautions may have to extend to family members.

Employees have a right to be informed about known occupational health hazards. They also have a right to enjoy comparable health and safety standards, regardless of location. Employees should inform themselves about potential hazards at their intended destination and take the necessary precautions.

Travel health assessments should be conducted on personnel who will be traveling or living abroad. These assessment should include the following elements:

- review of the specific health requirements for the country of destination
- review of the health risks for that country
- immunization as required
- medical travel advice and personal health protection
- "fitness to travel" assessment

4.8.1 MEDICAL ASSISTANCE GROUPS

Many entities provide their travelers with access to medical assistance through an international medical plan, use of a medical assistance group, or a combination of both. In organizations with an international medical plan alone, the individual is responsible for coordinating coverage and submitting claims to the appropriate organization.

A private medical assistance group is a cost-effective way to obtain medical service in the style of a traveler's home country. For instance, a traveler from a Western country may not be accustomed to Eastern-style health services or sanitary standards. Medical assistance groups maintain databases of qualified delivery locations and in some cases operate their own medical clinics.

These assistance groups also provide interim medical advice by phone. An example might be a traveler who has severe diarrhea in his hotel room. The traveler might be able to forgo medical treatment by following basic medical steps given by the service, might receive a visit in his room from a doctor, or might be stabilized while transport is arranged.

The medical assistance group may also provide travelers with the following additional services (Institute of Business Travel Management & National Business Travel Association, 2003):

- help in overcoming language barriers
- monitoring progress during treatment and recovery
- communication support with family, business, and personal physicians
- management of medically necessary evaluations and transfers, or repatriation of remains
- facilitation of hospital admission
- coordination of guarantee or direct payments to health care providers
- coordination of the transfer of emergency blood, vaccines, and medications or lost or stolen prescriptions
- arrangement of the return of an employee's unattended dependent children to their place of residence
- transportation for family members or others who need to reach the sick or injured employee

Employees should be prepared to deal with major medical emergencies, such as injuries from traffic accidents. Personnel who will be doing extensive road travel in moderate- to high-risk countries should consider carrying a vehicle first aid kit, as well as their own plasma or blood.

The contingency plan and procedures should note the locations of international travel clinics to treat travelers or expatriates who are injured or become ill while abroad.

Upon returning home, employees should have access to a post-travel health assessment (PTA), especially when health status may have changed while traveling or exposure to infectious disease may have occurred.

4.8.2 IMMUNIZATIONS AND MEDICAL HISTORY

Deployment to international locations must consider the health of the assignee, from both immunization and emergency perspectives. Recommendations are available from the World Health Organization (www.who.int), the U.S. Centers for Disease Control and Prevention (www.cdc.gov), and the British National Travel Health Network and Centre (www.nathnac.org). Each supplies timely, accurate information about health challenges in various countries.

The book *CDC Health Information for International Travel 2010* serves as a guide to the practice of travel medicine and is the authoritative source of U.S. government recommendations for immunizations and prophylaxis for foreign travel.

Travelers can better protect themselves by traveling with enough prescription medicines, carrying appropriate medical records, and understanding the level of medical support at the destination.

4.9 SECURITY AWARENESS TRAINING

Knowledge is power, whether in the hands of a facility manager, a traveler, or family members deployed with an expatriate. Awareness programs for traveling employees should include hints for personal security while walking, using public transportation, driving, traveling by travel, and staying in hotels.

Training should also address the protection of proprietary information. Employees traveling abroad often possess proprietary information that has economic value. Locals may try to obtain that information. Encryption and other protective methods may be necessary.

Awareness programs should also address dealing with local authorities. Bribes are often demanded at border crossings, and the traveling employee must be educated on the best way to deal with local officials. Employees must also be warned of the consequences of becoming involved with drugs or prostitution in foreign countries.

In some cases, travelers may require comprehensive travel instructions. These are often best provided in the form of a booklet, which could address the following:

- identification of the risks
- preparation (medical, travel documents, etc.)
- appropriate clothing to take on the trip because of environmental or religious requirements
- what to do on arrival (transportation issues, embassy and consulate contacts, etc.)
- dealing with border authorities
- precautions in the country of destination
- crime
- what to do if arrested or incarcerated
- what to do in the event of illness or accident
- what to do in the event of a natural disaster or political upheaval
- telephone contacts in the country of destination and at home

4.9.1 EMBASSIES AND CONSULATES

Personnel should be provided with the numbers and addresses for the embassies and consulates nearest to their destination. Some countries allow for Web-based registration of resident travelers so they can be located by their government in an emergency.

4.9.2 CULTURE ORIENTATION

As business expands across the globe, global awareness and cross-border business skills are more important than ever. Classroom and online cultural awareness training helps travelers and expatriates increase their knowledge, skills, and strategies for working and surviving globally. Such training can help them

- understand cultural differences and their day-to-day impact on business,
- improve cross-cultural communication, resulting in fewer conflicts, misunderstandings, and potentially costly mistakes, and
- understand the potential for fraud, abuse, and corruption as a way of doing business in some countries.

4.9.3 EMPLOYEE PROFILE AND EMERGENCY INFORMATION

A personal profile is a collection of personal information that may be useful when an employee is traveling abroad or if he or she is kidnapped. Data to be collected includes required medications, medical conditions, physician contact, blood type, and distinguishing marks and scars. Data from the profile can help in determining whether a threat is real or a hoax and may also be useful in investigating the incident and formulating a response. With the profile in place, there is a better chance of a successful rescue.

For moderate- to high-risk countries, a profile should be completed and stored in a sealed envelope marked as follows:

Personal Profile [Name] To be opened only in the event of an emergency

Some companies collect fingerprints, handwriting and printing exemplars, voice recordings, and secret passwords.

An example of a personal profile is found in this chapter's appendix.

4.9.4 EMPLOYEE AND ASSET TRACKING

Global positioning system (GPS) tracking of employees and assets can be helpful for both piece of mind and recovery.

4.9.5 CARRIER SAFETY ANALYSIS

Aircraft and watercraft throughout the world are not regulated by a central organization. Some countries' carriers are more prone to problems due to maintenance, training, and personnel deficiencies. Some firms review these carriers and rate their air- or sea-worthiness in general.

4.9.6 GROUND TRANSPORTATION

Road travel in some locations is challenging and dangerous. Businesses must assess the risk of various forms of transportation for their employees.

Examples of ground transportation concerns are as follows:

- **Taxis.** Should a single female be allowed to take a taxi?
- **Rental cars.** Should a traveler from a right-hand-drive country be able to rent a vehicle in a left-hand-drive country?
- **Public transport.** Should a traveler be allowed to ride a train in a developing country?

A good resource on road transportation is the Association for Safe International Road Travel (www.asirt.org).

4.9.7 RESIDENCE AND HOTEL VETTING

Travelers to foreign lands have many considerations when vetting a hotel or residence. Is the area safe from a security perspective? Are proper controls in place?

Security practitioners must understand local safety issues. Is adequate medical response available? Are smoke detectors installed? Is a fire brigade nearby?

Safety hazards may pose a greater risk than security threats. For example, in developing countries the risk of fire (due to heating methods and inadequate building standards) can be significant.

4.9.8 DOMESTIC HELP VETTING

The use of domestic labor for housekeeping, babysitting, driving, and other support functions is common in some countries. Domestic help should be vetted carefully. When possible, it is advantageous to use workers who have previously (and successfully) served other expatriates.

4.10 PLANT AND OFFICE PHYSICAL SECURITY

Physical security controls for plant and office operations may be affected by unreliable power in the developing world. Even scheduled brownouts may affect access control, alarm, and closed-circuit television systems.

4.11 TELECOMMUTING

Allowing employees to work from home is a benefit to the employee and cost-effective for the employer, but it presents security challenges.

When expatriate employees telecommute from hotels or their homes abroad, they should follow a strict policy of physical and cyber security.

4.12 SUPPLY CHAIN DUE DILIGENCE

In today's global business environment, companies depend on other organizations all over the world. A global security practitioner must therefore ensure that the organization's international strategic partners employ satisfactory safeguards.

4.13 PREEMPLOYMENT BACKGROUND CHECKS AND DRUG TESTING

Other sections of *Protection of Assets* outline the standard approach to creating and implementing a comprehensive preemployment screening policy. However, in some parts of the world, databases containing criminal records are not digitized, are not centralized, or are nonexistent. Fraud—regarding criminal records, employment history, credentialing, and education—complicates the matter.

Privacy laws may tightly control the dissemination and use of records. The security practitioner should work closely with human resources personnel to understand what data is available, how reliable it may be, and how it can be employed in the hiring process.

The same challenges hold true for the use of drug and psychological testing. The practitioner must research the legality of the testing with regard to employment.

4.14 KIDNAP/RANSOM/EXTORTION RESPONSE

Many companies that deploy personnel to dangerous areas purchase a kidnap/ransom/ extortion (KR&E) insurance. KRE policies typically provide coverage for the following (Saul, 2009):

- ransom and extortion payments as a result of a kidnapping or extortion threat
- loss of the ransom or extortion payment while it is being delivered
- fees and expenses for independent negotiators, as well as travel and accommodation expenses
- political threat coverage for expenses when a person is wrongfully detained by anyone acting for a government or with the government's approval

Extortion is defined as a threat, made in conjunction with a ransom demand, to perform an act such as the following:

- killing, injuring, or abducting a person
- damaging property or contaminating products
- divulging trade secrets
- introducing a computer virus

Other expenses, such as these, may also be covered:

— reward to informant
— cost of temporary security measures recommended by certified company
— fees for a public relations consultant
— fees for an interpreter
— salaries of employees assisting in negotiations
— personal financial loss due to the physical inability to attend to personal financial matters

— interest on loans raised to meet insured loss
— settlements and judgments imposed on the insured by or on behalf of a covered person or stockholders as a direct result of extortion

Corporations usually keep their KR&E coverage confidential to avoid being targeted.

4.15 BRIBERY AND CORRUPTION

In some countries bribery and corruption are accepted both culturally and legally. Transparency International (www.transparency.org), which bills itself as "the global coalition against corruption," publishes its Corruption Perception Index annually. The index is a tool that can help a security practitioner gauge the risks in a particular country. In addition, the Eastern Michigan University College of Business (www.cob.emich.edu) provides Web links for researching international bribery and corruption.

Some countries' laws address the conduct of their citizens regardless of where they are. For example, the Foreign Corrupt Practices Act (FCPA) in the United States makes it unlawful for a U.S. person to make a payment to a foreign official for the purpose of obtaining or retaining business for or with, or directing business to, any person. In the United Kingdom, anti-bribery laws were strengthened with the Bribery Act of 2010.

Security practitioners must be aware of these laws and their potential impact on the organizations they support. Security can help the organization by arranging for or providing investigations into potential suppliers, joint venture partners, or other entities that may have a business relationship with the company.

4.16 INFORMATION SECURITY

Rapid changes in information technology call for special efforts in protecting information assets abroad. In some countries, sufficiently protective laws and regulations may not exist. Many corporations have to rely on contractual law for remedy when a business partner suffers loss or intrusion.

Traveling across borders with information, be it written or digital, may expose the information to review. Employees should not expect information privacy when traveling abroad. In fact, when analyzing the risk of doing business in a particular country, it makes sense to consider the country's cultural and legal stance on the protection of intellectual property, as well as the country's propensity to attempt to gather information through electronic means.

In addition, other countries may not have, or may not enforce, laws against wiretapping. The security manager may have to arrange for regular electronic countermeasures (anti-eavesdropping) sweeps of offices or hotel rooms where business is being conducted. Telecommunications are especially susceptible to eavesdropping, and employees should be encouraged not to use telephones (landline or mobile) or faxes for confidential information. Personnel traveling with laptop computers may be able to use encryption software to protect electronically transferred documents. (The security manager should ensure that the type of encryption being employed can legally be used in the destination country.) Satellite telephones may also provide an increased level of security for communications to the home base.

The global economy presents unique challenges for security practitioners. They need to act as holistic risk managers, constantly monitoring, evaluating, and adjusting as needed, and they must be prepared to manage an issue from anywhere.

APPENDIX A

CONFIDENTIAL PERSONAL PROFILE

This form is for the use of those traveling to selected international locations. It should be completed and sealed in a confidential envelope and forwarded to Security. The information will then be available in the event of an emergency. Please attach a recent photograph and a set of fingerprints of all family members if applicable.

Date ____________________

EMPLOYEE INFORMATION

Name (last) ________________ (first) ____________________ (known as) ______________________

Permanent residence ____

Phone ____

Secondary residence ____

Phone ____

Physical description

Height __________________ Weight ____________________ Eyes ____________________

Hair ____________________________________ Date of birth ______________________

Scars/marks ____

Critical medication ____

Doctor (name and contact #) ____

FAMILY INFORMATION

Spouse or domestic partner

Name (last) ________________ (first) ____________________ (known as) ______________________

Employer ____

Address ____

Phone ____

Physical description

Height __________________ Weight ____________________ Eyes ____________________________

Hair ______________________________________ Date of birth ______________________________

Scars/marks ____

Critical medication ____

Doctor (name and contact #) ____

Children or others in household

Name	Date of birth	Height	Weight	Eyes

1. ____
2. ____
3. ____
4. ____

If applicable, attach further information.

Family cars

1. Driver ____

   Make ____

Year ______________________ Model ______________________

Color ______________________ License ______________________

2. Driver ______________________

Make ______________________

Year ______________________ Model ______________________

Color ______________________ License ______________________

3. Driver ______________________

Make ______________________

Year ______________________ Model ______________________

Color ______________________ License ______________________

Contacts who will have knowledge of the family members' whereabouts

Name Address Phone

1. ______________________
2. ______________________
3. ______________________
4. ______________________
5. ______________________
6. ______________________

Additional information on children or other household members

1. Name ______________________

   School attended ______________________

   Resident or day student (circle) ______________________

School address ______________________________

Phone ______________________________

Employer ______________________________

Employer address ______________________________

Phone ______________________________

2. Name ______________________________

School attended ______________________________

Resident or day student (circle) ______________________________

School address ______________________________

Phone ______________________________

Employer ______________________________

Employer address ______________________________

Phone ______________________________

3. Name ______________________________

School attended ______________________________

Resident or day student (circle) ______________________________

School address ______________________________

Phone ______________________________

Employer ______________________________

Employer address ______________________________

Phone ______________________________

4. Name ______________________________

School attended ______________________________

Resident or day student (circle) ______________________________

School address ______________________________

Phone ______________________________

Employer ______________________________

Employer address ______________________________

Phone ______________________________

Handwriting sample

Please write the following in your normal handwriting:

Dear Zach,

Well, the old class of "16" is through at last. You ask where the boys are to be. Val Brown goes on the 24th to Harvard for law. Don't forget to address him as "Esquire." Ted Updyke takes a position with the N. Y. W. H. & H. R. R., 892 Ladd Ave., Fall River, Massachusetts, and Jack McQuade with the D. L. & W. at Jersey City, N. J. 400 E. 6th Street. William Fellows just left for a department position in Washington; his address is 735 South G. St. At last account, Dr. Max King was to go to John Hopkins for a Ph.D. degree. Think of that! Elliott goes to Xenia, Ohio, to be a Y. M. C. A. secretary. I stay here for the present. What do you do next? How about Idaho?

Very truly yours,

(Signature of writer)

REFERENCES

iJet Intelligent Risk Systems. (2009). *Travel risk management maturity model*. Alexandria, Virginia: National Business Travel Association.

Institute of Business Travel Management & National Business Travel Association. (2003). *Emergency guidelines & procedures for corporate travel programs.* Available: http://www.travelrisk center.com/TRC/trc_files/Kroll_Crisis_Plan.pdf [2011, October 1].

Saul, D. (2009, September). Kidnap, ransom and extortion policy. *AGL*. Available: http:www.agl-mag.com [2011, October 1].

INDEX

A

access control, 53, 56, 68, 69, 73, 84, 100
accidents, auto, 120, 124
arrest, travel risk, 119, 125

B

background investigation, 114, 128
barriers, 30, 55, 76, 78, 96, 107
bombs, 28, 55, 77, 100, 108
briefings, general intelligence, 121
briefings, threat-specific, 121
building hours, 67, 85
buildings, closed, 67
buildings, hybrid, 67
buildings, open, 67

C

CCTV. See video surveillance
codes, building, 51, 57, 65, 72, 79
codes, fire, 51, 57, 62, 79
command center, 62, 95, 97, 99, 104, 106
communication at special event, 94, 97, 105, 107
communication in high-rise structure, 53, 54, 62
contamination of air, 53, 54
contamination of water, 53, 54
contingency planning. See crisis management
corruption, 114, 126, 130
country risk categories, 115, 121
crime, travel risk, 116, 117, 119
crisis management, 100, 114, 121, 122
crowd management, 34, 92, 95, 96, 106
culture, traveler's understanding of, 114, 119, 126

D

dogs, apprehension by, 32, 34, 35, 47
dogs, deployment, 29
dogs, diseases, 8, 11, 15
dogs, drug detection, 28, 38, 39, 40, 44
dogs, explosive detection, 28, 38, 39, 40, 44
dogs, feeding, 9, 14, 26
dogs, handlers, 4, 6, 9, 21, 26, 29, 31, 32, 36, 38
dogs, herding, 2
dogs, in military, 2
dogs, inspection of, 9, 10
dogs, instinctive drives, 3, 7, 25, 36
dogs, intelligence, 4, 21, 23, 38
dogs, kennels, 8, 18, 20
dogs, liability, 30, 34, 45, 48, 49
dogs, patrol, 28, 30, 32, 34, 48
dogs, precautions, 34, 48
dogs, searching with, 3, 6, 28, 33, 34, 36, 38, 41, 42, 44
dogs, senses, 3, 23, 26, 33, 36, 44
dogs, surveillance, 34
dogs, tracking, 33, 36, 38, 44
dogs, training, 2, 3, 4, 6, 15, 22, 24, 28, 29
dogs, working, 1, 15
domestic help, vetting, 128
duress alarms, 83

E

elevators, 52, 64, 67, 69, 70, 71, 73, 77, 80, 84
embassies, 118, 125
emergency planning for high-rise structure, 53, 56, 62, 63, 65, 79, 86
equipment, security, 55, 83, 96, 98, 106, 107
evacuation, from abroad, 114, 120, 121
evacuation, of building, 52, 56, 62, 63, 86, 96, 101
event locations, 95
event planning, key factors in, 93, 95, 99
event schedule, 97, 106

event security director, 94, 96, 99
expatriates, 112, 115, 124, 126, 128

F

fire alarm systems, 56, 57, 58, 59, 79
fire extinguishment, 8, 59, 60
fire in high-rise structures, 51, 52, 53, 56, 57, 58, 59
first aid, 117, 118, 120, 123, 124

G

ground transportation, 114, 121, 127

H

hardening, site, 76, 77
heat detectors, 58
high-rise structure, definition, 51
hotels, vetting, 114, 127

I

illness, travel risk, 120, 125
information security, 94, 131
insurance, kidnap/ransom/extortion, 129
insurance, medical/evacuation, 114, 123
intelligence, travel, 113, 121
intrusion alarms, 65, 72, 74, 75, 76, 82, 83

J

K

kidnapping, 101, 119, 126, 129

L

life safety in high-rise structures, 52, 53, 55, 56, 63, 65, 79
lighting, security, 76
local national employees, 112, 120
locks, 56, 59, 72, 73, 78, 80

M

medical assistance groups, 120, 123
medical issues abroad, 114, 116, 117, 120, 123, 124, 126
medical issues at special events, 95, 99, 101, 104, 105, 107

N

natural disasters, 63, 120, 122, 125
notification of fire or emergency services, 62
notification of occupants, 62

O

operations center, 95, 97, 99, 105, 106

P

personnel living abroad. See expatriates
policies, 76, 83, 86, 93, 97, 100, 105, 108, 112, 114, 117, 122
post assignments, 85, 100, 105, 106
profile, personal (travelers), 114, 117, 126, 132

Q

R

residences, vetting, 127
risk assessment, 52, 93, 108, 114, 117
Risk Self-Assessment Tool (DHS), 94, 108

S

security awareness training, 93, 118, 119, 125
security personnel, 70, 85, 94, 95, 99, 104, 105
security systems, integrated, 73, 85
smoke control, 54, 58, 60, 62, 80
smoke detection, 58, 73, 127
sprinkler systems, fire, 8, 53, 58, 59, 62
stairwells, 52, 56, 62, 68, 71, 77, 79, 82
standpipes, 58
supply chain, 120, 128

T

telecom protection, building, 65, 74, 76
telecommuting, 128
travel health assessment, 117, 123, 124
travelers, 114, 115, 117, 125, 132

U

V

video surveillance, 65, 71, 74, 76, 83, 84, 95
Vulnerability Identification Self-Assessment Tool (DHS), 93, 108

W

weather, impact on special events, 98, 99, 101

XYZ